Eyes of God

Expand Your Vision, Revolutionize Your Life

by Linda LaFlamme

.

Eyes of God

Expand Your Vision,
Revolutionize Your Life

The author of this book does not dispense medical advice or prescribe the use of any technique as a form of treatment for physical, emotional, or medical problems without the advice of a physician, either directly or indirectly. The intent of the author is only to offer information of a general nature to help readers in their quest for emotional and spiritual growth and well-being. In the event that you use any of this information in this book for yourself, which is your constitutional right, the author and publisher assume no responsibility for your actions.

Printed in the United States of America

First Printing: December 2014

Published by Starfire Multimedia LLC

Starfire Multimedia books may be purchased for educational, business, spiritual, or sales promotional use. For information please write: Special Markets Department, Starfire Multimedia LLC, 2675 W State Route 89A #1088, Sedona, AZ 86336 USA.

Library of Congress Cataloging-in-Publication Data
Library of Congress Control Number: 2014921299
Starfire Multimedia LLC, Sedona, AZ USA

LaFlamme, Linda

Eyes of God : Expand Your Vision, Revolutionize Your Life / Linda LaFlamme. – 1st ed.,.
p. cm.

ISBN: 978-0-9960601-0-3
Digital ISBN: 978-0-9960601-1-0

STARFIRE
MULTIMEDIA LLC

Eyes of God

Expand Your Vision, Revolutionize Your Life

by

Linda LaFlamme

STARFIRE MULTIMEDIA LLC

Eyes of God

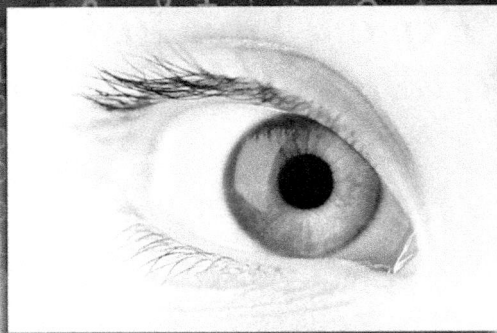

Expand Your VISION
Revolutionize Your Life

by Linda LaFlamme

Dedication, Loving Thanks, and Acknowledgements

This book is dedicated to <u>you</u>. May you realize the full beauty inside of you, your essence, and see that loving radiance surround you. Realize who you are... and share that beauty and your unique gifts with the world. Shine your brilliance!

~

I have great love in my heart and gratitude for my wonderful friends, colleagues, associates and partners for shining their brilliance in this world. I would like to thank those special people who have helped this project take wings, specifically my incredible team including Rama, Denise, Tom, Char, La Rae, and Tonya. My most amazing friends and supporters. To loving Lillian, a shining presence. To my extended fabulous family. For my parents, my mom and dad who were a true source of fire-inspiration. Just carrying the torch.

And to everyone who has ever graced my life... past, present and future - you know who you are. And I love you eternally.

Table of Contents

Introduction

Dare to be different. Dare to be you. You may be a thought leader or an entrepreneur. Or a student of life. You may be a parent who is raising evolved beings. You may be at the beginning or may be well on your way on your life's path. Whatever your orientation or point of focus, my desire is for you to experience the most joyful journey in your time here on this planet and to create your best life adventure possible. To be the hero in your own delicious story.

I humbly thank you for reading this book as it was inspired to be written for you, the progressive, intelligent and brilliant soul that *you* are.

In reading this book you will learn how visionaries and luminaries find new ideas and see them into being, into reality. You will learn the process of how your inner vision from your mind's eye creates the world that you see and experience, and how your actual vision from your eye/brain system correlates to your life experiences and to the quality of your life. You will learn how to make any desired changes or course corrections to head in the direction of reaching your destined path, the one that is calling to you with the most joy and potential. After completing this book, you will have the knowledge of how to expand your vision to include new thought trajectories into areas of your greatest desires and talents, you will learn how to release old habits and patterns that do not serve you, and you will learn how to *see* with more clarity and experience your life from a bold, beautiful color palette, as if with new eyes. Your Eyes of God.

You will learn that what we see and experience in the outside world is a projection of our inner world.

Our early lives, and very often our entire lives, are based on how we *learned to see*. We can expand our vision to create the best and most delicious lives possible.

Our external technology mirrors our human technology. We as humans begin life as Recorders and then become adult Projectors, creating our individual experiences. We are here to create and to evolve our human species family patterns and circumstance, and our world, with our desired and inspired thoughts. We envision these thoughts into being. And then we see them.

We are seven billion people here experiencing seven billion different worlds. We all write our own scripts to the stories of our lives. We are creators. And evolvers. We are all the Eyes of God.

Preface

The initial seed idea for this book came to me over twenty years ago. I was in my home near Boston and had purchased a stone with some script writing on it that read "Create Your Own Reality". I stared at this stone for some time and knew, deep inside, that I would be on a journey to explore the how's and why's of this statement. Was this really true - that we could create our own reality? My reality in my very early life was not really all that pleasant. It was pretty horrible for long stretches, quite frankly. A few times I angrily put the stone in a drawer, scoffing at the idea and the audacity of the thought that we could create our own reality here. If so, why would I have chosen this circumstance? What about those who were even less fortunate? But then, over time... the stone seemed to call out to me, beckoning me to re-explore this idea. I didn't realize at the time that this would become part of my life's work. But then again, we never do, right? We just create our experiences as we go, and then at some point we see the fabric of what we have created. The beautiful tapestry of our lives. Our lives may take twists and turns, but it makes the journey all that much sweeter when we finally "see" our tapestry, the cloth of many colors, with new eyes, eyes of wisdom and grace. That only life experience can bring.

Just prior to writing this book I kept repeatedly noticing a particular type of majestic flowering desert plant when I would hike or drive up the canyon near my home. They would seem to call out to me to look at them as though they had a message to convey. Observing these captivating creatures blooming in Sedona inspired me to learn more about them. These are a type of agave, sometimes called Century plants around here. This particular type of agave lives 10-30 years and they bloom in only the last year of their life. At that point they send up a flower stalk with big yellow flowers that can reach 25-30 feet high (8-9 meters) towards the sky. They seemed to have a message for me and I took it as a sign, as a reminder, that this was time to put my thoughts down in writing. My thoughts about creating our own reality. This is a culmination of one part of my journey, as I am entering a new chapter of my life, a new way of being. After learning about the century plants, I began to gaze at these blossoming wonders with honor whenever I drove or hiked by them, communicating back to them, "Great job, you have grown a beautiful flower of wisdom. Your life has been rich and we who pass by appreciate your time here and the beautiful knowledge that you are emanating".

We are all here to share and to grow and to bloom. The wisdom gained on our journeys is to be radiated and appreciated. The wrinkles show our character and that we are wiser than we were before. Evolution is an inside job. Always enjoy the journey. The journey of you.

My wish for you is to create the best life possible. We all want different things and have come to this planet for different experiences. There are no right or wrong answers or paths. Only our true path. And you know this by your passion, your drive, and what you feel in your heart and deep in your soul. You are here to enjoy your life and to create the best journey possible. My hope is that you find some inspiration within the words and between the words of this book. And that you go forth and create the life of your dreams. Right here and in the present, as that is all we ever have. I wish you the sweetest journey and life adventure. The life you desire. You are a creator. Go forth and create your best life!

Much love to you, Linda

CHAPTER 1
Vision Aspects and Angles

There are many different ways of looking at, of seeing, the world. Of experiencing the world. What we see in the outside world is a reflection of our inner world.

What do you see?

What would you like to see?...

~

We are a planet of over seven billion humans living in seven billion unique worlds. All placed into being here by something greater, a power greater than our individual points of focus.

Who is that power? What is that power? The power that creates universes. That creates us. Why are we here? How significant are we as individual beings? Why are *you* here? Why do *you* exist?

We'll explore the answers to these questions and your individual path in our time together here. I am so happy that you are joining me on this unfolding journey. The journey of you. I know you will be so delighted with what you uncover. The jewel within. You. In all of your glory.

Just as it was meant to be.

But first, to best understand this process let's review how we as humans develop and create, maneuver, manipulate, dodge, hide, seek, see, explore and experience this world of ours.

There are many ways of looking at the world. Of seeing the world. Our experience of life here is as different and unique as each one of us is, each of our individual points of view. These are developed into being by our familial learned behaviors and patterns, habits, thoughts, and our life experiences. Also our individual talents, gifts, desires and path we travel upon, and the decisions we make about which road we take in life.

As you look out in the world, what do you see?

Some see a world of joy and love, a world of caring, family and community. Some see a world of strife, lack, depression or hardship. Many of us see a combination of all of the above.

We all have a different perspective and orientation. The Indian parable of the elephant comes to mind. There are six men who all touch a different part of the elephant; the trunk, tusk, side, tail, ear, and leg. They all describe the elephant in a different way. And they all experience the elephant in a different way. And they all think they are right. *And they are!* But they all have a limited perspective of the elephant. They can only see part of him.

And this is how it goes with us. We see and experience life, people, places, things, events ...and ourselves... from our habitual limited viewpoint, one small point of focus. We have been standing in a particular spot with a particular vantage point, unable to see more of the larger picture.

We will explore how to do just that. My hope for you is that by the end of this part of our journey together, this book, you will see from a larger vantage point than you do now, even if your vantage point now is quite expansive. And we all think that our vantage point is the biggest it can be ...until we see beyond.

There are almost infinite levels of seeing, of understanding. And it is all within you. Right here and right now.

Just as you began life in your physical body as a "meeting of the minds" of DNA and a small and multiplying mass of cells. These cells had all of the knowledge to keep expanding into greater complexity and expression to create organs, systems, specialized functions, and ultimately a full human body in all of its intricate and amazing expression. These original cells possessed the wisdom of you - unfolding in the perfect time

The perfect time is now for you to continue to expand your vision horizon and to further realize your true brilliance. The time is now as you have desired to read this book. And you have called this book through me. This was written for _you_.

Different Vantage Points

We as humans are each a different point of focus. A point of focus within a specific time. With a locus, a specific location. All seeing from our very own special angle.

And as a group, different generations have different vantage points. A generation was born within a specific social and societal milieu or background.

If we relate this to our elephant example, we can see that even within the same generation we may have vastly different experiences of what life is like here on earth. All different ways of seeing and describing the metaphorical elephant.

For example, in the 1960s in the USA in particular, there was a period of social unrest, a period of high-fueled growth, of revolution in the air.

In this same time frame in other countries around the globe, people were experiencing yet different vantage points, points of focus, desires for their world, and different social ideals.

In the 1800s life looked very different than the 20th century. And no internet... *Imagine!*

Throughout history there has always been a quest forward, one of exploration, one of desiring freedom. Freedom of speech, freedom from oppression, to express on greater levels. One of desiring connection with nature and with other humans. One of improving our lives and the lives of future generations. These are constants in our collective journey forward.

Each time period of history had and has its own story and soundtrack. Moving forward with its specific tempo and storyline. Moving *us* forward.

We live in a world of our own experience. All Eyes of God. Looking at and experiencing life here. Creating a better world.

Where do you live now? What does your world look like? Where do you want to live?

What does *that* world look like?

Heaven and Hell

Life is what you make of it. It is what you see and how you see it, your perception, your perspective, your vantage point. Mathematically speaking it is your angle. Your point of view. ...You are a point on a line. On a grid really.

In the Buddhist tradition, there exists the story of Indra's Net, describing the jewels at each intersection of the net, reflecting the other jewels.

5

As you look out in the world, what do you see?

I suppose your answer would depend upon the direction that you are looking toward. And from which vantage point you are looking from.

If you are looking in the direction of and looking for problems, disease, discomfort, and disempowerment, then that is what you will see.

If you are looking from the vantage point of being in the world and seeing poverty, hunger, injustice, hard work, effort, struggle, lack, some outside force keeping you down, then that is where your focus resides, at the moment, and that is what you will experience or continue to experience.

When you are "in the trenches" you are in the trenches at that point on a grid. This is what you see, this is what you know, this is what you live day-to-day, this is your experience of life. This is how you could define life, as it surrounds, permeates and moves through and in you. *And I know, I've been there.*

There are levels of understanding of life, other points on the grid. To get ourselves out the trenches, or out of a seeming bottomless pit of hell, you must "rise above it" as has been stated by many oppressed peoples. They (you) have the wisdom to rise above anything that you do not wish to experience any longer.

There is a physics to life here on earth. Everything really is math, at its base level vibration. Angles, points, lines, formulas, equations ...

And it is also emotion, feeling, vision, desire, love and joy.

Mathematics is the container for the essence of life, which is our passions and desires, feelings and emotions. It provides the framework and structure where we reside and experience life.

> *Heaven on earth. Seen through the Eyes of God.*
> *Over seven billion viewing angles.*

But how and why do we have these various angles and points of view? Why are they so vastly different? Can we change our point of view?

Human Technology

There is a brilliant design to human beings. And external technology in our world is a mirror to our human technology.

As human beings we go through several stages of metamorphoses to become the latest and greatest revised highest technological edition of ourselves. Lean, mean computing machines.

First we begin life as Recorders. We are born into a world and we record impressions throughout our growing years. These form the basis of our internal program. We are programmed with a certain software and even in a certain language. After our growing years we move to the next phase of our human technological development, and we morph from a Recorder into a Projector. Let's discuss this in further detail...

Recorders

When we are born and through our growing and developing years we are like Recorders. We record the experiences around us. We learn, yes by words and instruction, but more by example and through observing behavior of those around us. We learn to an even greater degree by the energetic environment that we are in, which is the mindset of our families, circumstances, peers, generation and community.

We are born at a locus, a point in time and place. The energy and thought of this point becomes our focus. It has a specific meaning to us. As a Recorder, we receive and absorb. We interpret by how we feel. We don't distinguish whether or not the information either offered directly or by osmosis, is accurate or correct. We don't yet have a reference point to make that determination, so we cannot. At our growing stage of development as humans our human technology is primarily read-write. We are Recorders, we are observers and receivers. Not full creators of our worlds... yet. Our young lives leave indelible impressions on us.

You may think that we are bound by the luck of the draw. Where we are born, to which circumstances we are born into, to whom. Our race, gender, affluence or lack thereof, loving environment or lack thereof. All of these we cannot change.

But they serve as the basis for us to create our best lives. You'll see how as we go forward...

But first, let's explore how we arrive at our individual points of view. Our beliefs, proclivities, and patterns.

Education In and Out

It is always heartwarming for me to hear stories such as that of Palmer Luckey, the homeschooled teen who invented the Oculus Rift and founded the company Oculus VR, which was sold for $2B when he was age 21. Or Bill Gates who dropped out of Harvard to create a world-changing company. Same for Mark Zuckerberg. And brilliant inventors and creators such as Elon Musk, Dean Kamen, Peter Diamandis and others who are bringing the future here to us now. These luminaries embody clear, expanded, and evolved vision.

Education can come to us in many forms... formal schools, university, or sometimes even more importantly, from real world education, the school of life itself, when we can see beyond the current worldview in society, when we catch glimpses from our inner knowing, our inner guidance, the mind behind our Eyes.

Thought-Habit-Belief-Pattern (T-H-B-P)

We all have our unique set of beliefs. These were given to us by our parents, community, family lineage and society, relative to the time, place, location and milieu that we were born into.

Our beliefs and patterns create our worlds and how we experience life here. For example, if you believe that you can accomplish great things, then that will be how you experience life. If you believe that you are not worthy, nor smart, nor thin enough, or are inferior... then that is how you will experience your life.

However, our beliefs or patterns are not us. They are only a beginning point of reference and choice for us.

So how did we acquire our beliefs and patterns? Let's delve into this a little further....

You have a set of beliefs with you. These beliefs started out as a thought, usually that we were exposed to at home, in our communities, in our environments, through our media. We were exposed to a thought and then maybe even bombarded with it, in the case of advertising or media or news, or immersed in it, in the case of family, peers or community. But please know that these thoughts outside of you that you adopted - are not you. You have adopted them as your own, often by osmosis, and often without even realizing it, or questioning where they began. And if you never saw anything different that deviated from that thought, then you took it as gospel. When we are in the Recorder stage, when we are children and growing up, prior to adulthood, we are read-write. We do not have a reference point other than our milieu of what we are experiencing. We simply record it as the way we view the world as it is.

So it started as a thought, usually someone else's. Then you habitually began thinking it. In a sense you then adopted it as your own, but remember, it is still an outside thought that had nothing really to do with you, who you really are. Then, habit is a funny thing. We continue like an automaton to practice habits because either we are unaware of them or because they have become ingrained so we just continue to do them. Those around us may be doing them, even if they are destructive, so we think that this is how things are done or how things work. And remember, these mere thoughts which have now become habits, that started out as someone else's ideas, are not even yours. Now many are of value, and those you will want to keep, of course. Our parents put in a lot of effort into teaching us what they were taught as the best way that they knew (that were their habits and patterns). But there are some thoughts or habits that don't necessarily benefit you, some you don't need anymore. How do you know the difference? By the feeling of them. The feeling in your gut. The feeling in your heart. Your body does not lie. If you are doing something and it feels good to you, for example if you have a habit of eating healthy foods or exercising then your body will show you of its appreciation by functioning optimally. Indicators are stamina, well-being, and feelings of health. You feel good when you eat healthy and when you move your body.

If you have a habit that when you practice it does not feel good then maybe it's time to examine it. For example if you have a habit of gossiping about other people or diminishing other people, you know deep in your heart that this does not feel good. How would you feel if someone did this to you? Or if you have a habit of putting yourself down, feeling negative because you don't feel like you measure up to someone else's standards - how does that feel? Not good. And to think that this all started with an erroneous thought that wasn't even yours to begin with. Maybe its time to drop those habits that don't feel good that aren't even yours, aren't true and don't serve you.

As a step further, a habit that you keep doing for a long time then becomes a belief. A belief is just that and only that - a habit that first started as a thought, usually someone else's, that you have been doing for a while. Now, it is second nature to you and through the habit of thinking a particular thought, you have brought evidence of that thought to yourself through your emanations of it. And now it becomes a belief. You see it. And then you believe it.

T-H-B-P
Thought > Habit > Belief > Pattern

You continue to believe it because you have proven to yourself that it is true by your focus on it and hence attracting evidence of it.

As a small example, just as when you purchase a particular vehicle make and model and then you start seeing them everywhere. It is because your focus is on it, it has become a focal point for you, more so than other vehicle types. So you see it. You see more of what you focus on.

Thought-Habit-Belief-Pattern is persistent

After a period of time of believing something as true, it becomes seemingly more difficult to change it. You are more invested in it. You may even fight change on it. After all, it is a "belief" of yours. But, really, it is only a thought, usually someone else's, that you focused on and it became a habit. And now you have practiced it and are invested in it. So it became a belief. Now it becomes a pattern. A standing wave. An emanation of your personality, for better or worse. Thought - Habit - Belief - Pattern, T-H-B-P.

Which wouldn't be so bad, unless the patterns are self-defeating, destructive, or bring you the opposite of joy.

However...

You can change your beliefs at any time. As they are only thoughts that were not even yours to begin with. They are thoughts that you have been thinking for a period of time, perhaps a long time, perhaps even a lifetime. That is it. No more, no less. Just thoughts.

So, if you have a belief that this person or that person, or this group or that group is wrong about this or that, or that you are deficient in some way, it all started as a thought, that likely was someone else's, based on their own (mis)perceptions, that they then kept thinking whether through osmosis or laziness or lack of courage to break out and think their own thoughts, express themselves. Then they developed a habit of thinking this thought, And then it turned into a belief. And then they taught this belief to you. Which started out initially as an erroneous thought, a misperception. And now you have this pattern of behavior. Which actually started out as someone else's faulty thought.

All prejudices are learned.

All self-defeating thoughts and behaviors are learned.

That is, we were not born with these. We were exposed to something, somewhere down the line, that triggered this thought in us.

These erroneous and destructive thoughts are not you. What does not serve you, let go of.

If it serves you, keep it. If it doesn't serve you, toss it, release it.

You have the power to break any negative chains right now.

How? To start… by seeing differently, by allowing a new thought. One that feels good to <u>you</u>. Because the criteria for living your best, most joyful and satisfying life is thinking and feeling thoughts that feel good to you personally, and then creating your life to reflect your desires, where you can express yourself, your essence fully, in the ways that bring you the most pleasure and make the most sense to you.

Often though our systems and our signals have gotten confused from all of the chatter and misinformation that we have believed erroneously. This chatter that started out as another's misperceptions or projected thought, turned habit, turned by osmosis to your beliefs and then patterns.

If we grew up in a home that was emotionally, mentally or physically abusive, we may equate abuse with home or love. This is an example of a very large erroneous belief. This is why sometimes those that were abused go on to become abusers (pattern). It is because it's what they know, what they are familiar with, and they think that is how people act. It was an incorrect thought and projection from maybe generations ago, that was transferred through osmosis and finally to the newest child of that family.

As a child I remember looking at the world and wondering why evolution of thought had to be so slow. It seems that we live our lives and expect those that come after us to make the changes. This is incredibly slow and tedious and oftentimes not fun in the process as people work things out in a long and slow manner, creating similar experiences through habit of thought.

In reality there is only the <u>now</u>. Today. This is why you cannot make a resolution tomorrow. Because tomorrow actually never arrives. When you wake up in the morning, it is today. So if you say you are going to do something tomorrow, such as resolutions and cleaning out the garage, this means that you aren't doing it. And really, for greater joy and soul satisfying endeavors, why put off your best life for one more day? All it takes is an internal shift of thought. And it is much easier than you think.

There is no long arduous work involved. You don't have to effort in looking at how you first acquired those old beliefs, these may be disempowering beliefs about yourself, unhealthy habit patterns, and you could spend a lifetime unrolling all of that. Like slicing into a never-ending onion, peeling away the layers, while crying all along with each layer.

But the fact is, it doesn't even matter. What matters is that you live your best life today. Besides, looking at things that do not work only perpetuates said things that do not work. Because you are putting focus on it. As by putting energy into something that isn't working, cursing it, fighting it, looking continually at it, looking at the problem, you can never find the solution. There is no bottom to a problem. It is a point on a line. The lower you go or look vertically, plumbing the depths of the problem, you are still at the same point on the line. The point of the problem.

Or you may be in the now, at one point on a line, but looking backward at another. Using your vision to look backward at a point is using your vision to your disadvantage as you are looking backward not forward where you want to be. Because forward is the future that calls you, that beckons to you. It is your point of evolution.

To achieve a different result or a solution or a better situation, you need to engage with the problem in a different way, be it either personal or a world issue, you need to be at a different vantage point to have a different relationship with the problem.

Otherwise, you are perpetuating the problem as you are living it and focusing on that point on the line.

The only way to find the solution is to provide the milieu and probability for yourself to receive the solution. You cannot solve a problem from the same wavelength, the same vibrational level, the same point, where it lives. You must listen to your wisdom that calls and beckons you to the solution point. Or to the point of greater ease, knowledge, wisdom or joy.

> *"No problem can be solved from the same level of consciousness that created it."*
> *- Albert Einstein*

To do this you need to simply look within and feel your way to the solution. Whatever it is, ask yourself: How does it feel? How would it feel better? What would make my life relative to this thing or situation feel better, and then even better?

And then - now you have the new thought. Which can become a habit, belief and pattern. You then emanate to your family, your sphere of influence, your world, this new pattern, this new frequency of thought and being. This is how we evolve. This is how evolution works. You must allow yourself to go to that next logical point, to jump up to a greater level of understanding to view a situation from a different angle. This is how all great thinkers and visionaries (this includes you) have arrived at astounding new conclusions and places. This is the only way that new thoughts, habits, patterns, beliefs and ways of life come into being.

We arrived here into these lives, into our respective situations to read-write them as they are. We were meant to be Recorders at that stage. And our work here is to take *that*... and make it better. If you were not born into a particular situation that you felt gets an "N" for "Needs Improvement" you would not have the opportunity to make such a magnificent difference, a leap of evolution for yourself, for your family and lineage. And humankind as a whole.

So the choice is wallowing in the problem, whatever the problem may be, for weeks or years or generations, or looking at it tomorrow (and tomorrow never arrives), or choosing to think a new thought today.

And potentially change the world.

Field of Vision

As individual Eyes of God, we each have a field of vision that we literally see into, and from which we experience life, wrapped by the boundaries of that field. With our eyes/mind/brain system, we see items in front of us, to the sides, and in our peripheral vision. We see depth and can see items very close up or far away. We see better when there is more light rather than in darkness. And <u>we</u> shine the light.

Our vision with our eyes, which is unique to each of us, shows us how we individually view our world. Some of us are nearsighted, some are farsighted, some have very poor vision or clouded vision, while others have great vision. We live our lives metaphorically in this way also with varying degrees of visual clarity.

But just as with our eyes, we can improve our vision, see with greater acuity and clarity in life. This translates into seeing a bolder, better, and more colorful, clearer world. One that you want to see, one that is a joy to see. One that makes you excited to wake up each morning to greet each day that we are given here as a gift.

Perception

> *We see the world and express ourselves through the prism of our unique personalities.*

You are a point and have a point of view. All points of view are based on the information that one has collected and sifted through our marvelous brain. Our brain is like a computer. Or rather, computers were built on the model of the brain.

While our brain searches and connects with data to help create our experiences, our eyes function with our brain to help us see those experiences. Your lens of perception allows you to experience your world. We see the world and express ourselves through the prism of our unique personalities.

Your Field of Vision

We always must begin where we are at any point in time. And that is, right here and right now. You are likely reading this book because you innately know that you have a greater field of vision behind those eyes, your eyes, that is ready to be seen in the world. I know this too. It is my joyful hope that as we continue this journey together you will realize all of the brilliance inside of you. It is there. I see it. After all, *you* are in *my* field of vision, you are reading my book. I wrote this book for *you*.

Why have we discussed vision, how we see with our eyes, in the literal sense? Because how we see with our eyes relates to how we see in life. It relates to how we see our lives, how our realities look, and how we envision and create our lives.

Lies, Damn Lies, and Statistics

When I was in college, undergraduate studies, it was required to take several semesters of statistics. Which was cruel. But that's beside the point. In my first semester statistics class we were told to buy a book, *How to Lie with Statistics*, a classic. Not because the esteemed professor wanted us to lie with statistics, but to prove a point. And the point is this: Statistics can be made to say anything. Depending on our orientation and our perspective. And depending on <u>what we want to see</u>.

For example, we can read an imaginary headline, maybe from the 50s, that says:

A full 45% of all physicians in the US agree that smoking is cool.
or...
The majority of modern physicians strongly discourage smoking.
or...
Over 50% of physicians say "No" to smoking.
or...
83% of physicians who recommend smoking to relax, smoke Camels. Buy today!

Depending on how language is used, and what one is looking for, what one wants to see - whether they want to validate their smoking habit or to discourage their children from smoking, there is a study to prove it. It can even be the same study, worded differently in the context of agenda.

If you have something in your head, a thought, a particular point of view, you can do internet research and support whatever that point of view is. For example "Eating less fat is best for you", or "Eat more fats. Fats are important for your health". As another example, coffee (or tea or wine or milk or fill in the blank with a beverage of choice) is good for you. Or coffee (or tea or wine or milk or fill in the blank with a beverage of choice) is bad for you. This is true for endless subjects.

And if you have a dislike towards someone or something, you can always find others to commiserate with, who have the same dislike or complaining opinion, as you do.

You can find evidence to support any thought or belief that you may have.

Our result and experience is based on our outlook. The world is a safe and happy place to some. While the world is a scary, dog-eat-dog world to others. It is one's personal perspective. And this is often learned through osmosis at some point along the trail called your life.

Observer Effect

"The term *observer effect* refers to changes that the act of observation will make on a phenomenon being observed."[1]

The Pygmalion Effect and the Rosenthal Effect

"The Pygmalion effect, or Rosenthal effect, is the phenomenon whereby the greater the expectation placed upon people, the better they perform. The effect is named after the greek myth of Pygmalion. A corollary of the Pygmalion effect is the Golem effect, in which low expectations lead to a decrease in performance."[2]

This relates to our previous discussion, but is stated in another way. Our expectations create our reality and our experience. If we are working from a habit or pattern, then this is done for us without our conscious choice. If we choose what we want and expect, then this opens a whole new life experience for us, starting today.

When I was a small child, I remember my mother on occasions expecting me to misbehave. Even as a young child, I could see that she was creating a self-fulfilling prophecy. I could see that she was projecting onto me her own responses to a similar situation. And, frankly, I had not even thought of those responses, until she projected them and introduced them into my experience. Frustrated, I wanted to tell her, "Don't you see, you will create this. Your fear, this thing that you don't want to happen." But I didn't yet have the language to communicate that to her. And, I remember thinking, well if she expects me to act in a certain way, and she will not believe that I will act in a different way, then I may as well act in that way that she is projecting, as I am already untrusted and being punished for something I haven't even done yet. ... *And so it goes.*

When you expect the worst, you get the worst. Mountains out of molehills. When you expect the best, you get the best. You create the best.

The Pygmalion Effect is all about expecting the best and changing a reality to meet expectations. In my example above, had my mother expected me to act in the trajectory that I was naturally headed in, rather than expecting the worst, expecting and introducing a misbehavior into my experience, as an option, an expected option, then the outcome would have been different.

The Pygmalion Effect Relative to Schools
The Rosenthal - Jacobson Study

Robert Rosenthal and Lenore Jacobson (1968) report and discuss the Pygmalion effect in the classroom at length. In their study, they showed that if teachers were led to expect enhanced performance from some children, then the children did indeed show that enhancement.[3]

While we're on this topic, great teachers have tremendous impact on a child's life. Since we are Recorders when we are school-age, we absorb not only the lessons of school subjects taught eloquently, but absorb and process our teacher's responses to us as students and individuals. Who were some of your great teachers? I'll bet you still remember them, no matter what age you are at now. Their impact was that strong. Dedicated teachers, you are so very important in a child's life. I salute you!

These various effects and studies, Observer, Rosenthal, Pygmalion, Golem, are all another way of saying that we indeed do create what we are, we see what we want to see, what we think. We see what we are. It is all about vision. First our mental image, then our out-picturing as a result of what we are visioning inside of our minds.

You can apply this to business. And to all of life.

Placebo Effect

The Placebo Effect occurs when you take a course of action, a remedy or such, and you receive a positive effect, a benefit from it. But, ha-ha on you, the item itself was not the real treatment or drug or prescription.

This was developed as a way of scientific measure in double-blind studies to prove the efficacy of remedies. A way to measure if a medicine or drug was statistically helpful and effective or not.

As far as the Placebo Effect, it raises the question: Is the medicine, drug or thing introduced to your experience the cure? Or is it your mindset about the cure? Your belief that you can be cured? The strength of your desire to be cured?

The way I see it, if you think you can, you potentially can. If you think something will help you, it potentially may. If you do not think something will help you, then it potentially may not. Statistically speaking, of course.

It really is an individual path of perception and creation for each of us.

What is called The Placebo Effect is often people creating their results through their beliefs, their patterns of thought.

For the Placebo Effect or for "medicine" or a "solution" to actually work, you must have the wanting or the desire and the expectation on some level for healing or wholeness or return to health, believing that it is a possibility. We'll discuss in more detail further on. .. desire and expectation and belief.

What we see is a Reflection

Eyes of God. You. And Something Greater. Looking at the world.

If we are indeed the Eyes of God, then we create with our vision. We create what we see.

29

Chapter One:
Improve Your Vision ~
Vision Questions and Exercises

- Observe your reactions (your hot buttons) and your habits. These are old T-H-B-P. What are they? Are there any that don't benefit you? Do you need them still? Can you let them go?

- Make a list of patterns that do not serve your best interest. Recognizing those sets you free from them. Can you let these go?

- Now that you can "see" your patterns, and recognize others' patterns, you can choose a different thought and habit. What is your preferred way of living, what are the new thoughts, your new patterns that you would like to "see"?

- Review your old "recorder" list. What have you recorded, read-write, on your RAM that you don't need anymore in your now? Make a new list of desired outcomes with your new knowledge.

- Forgiveness... is releasing *yourself*. It is not about anyone else. Just ...let ...go. Look ahead. What do you want? Make that a focused thought. Think it into being.

  "The weak can never forgive. Forgiveness is the attribute of the strong." Mahatma Gandhi

CHAPTER 2
The World That We See

Definition of Vision

According to the Merriam-Webster Dictionary, the definition of VISION includes "a thought, concept, or object formed by the imagination", "a manifestation to the senses of something immaterial", "the act or power of imagination", "mode of seeing or conceiving", "unusual discernment or foresight", "the act or power of seeing, sight", and "something seen".[4]

What we see in the world, our worlds, is a reflection of how we see, our beliefs, what we see in our mind's eye, and our levels of connection with self and our inner vision. To fully understand vision and how it translates to a reality that we can see in the world, we need to understand how vision works and the process of seeing. Let's begin with a brief discussion of how our eyes translate and how we perceive our world. This is vision at its core and it would be helpful to remember these basic principles before going further on our journey. We won't take too long on this part, but it is essential.

Vision with Our Eyes, Our Eyesight

Different species on this earth have different types of eyes. There are ten different types of vision structures for differing species' use.

For example dragonflies have compound eyes, which are found in some insects and arthropods. Compound eyes have multiple lenses, and in the dragonfly's case, up to 1,000.

"Some compound eyes process an image in parallel, with each lens sending its own signal to the insect or arthropod's brain. This allows for fast motion detection and image recognition, which is one reason why flies are so hard to swat."[5]

Also, bees see differently than humans and see colors on the ultraviolet side of the spectrum that we cannot see.

Humans see only a small slice of the electromagnetic wavelength spectrum, which is the visible light portion. *See the diagram below.*

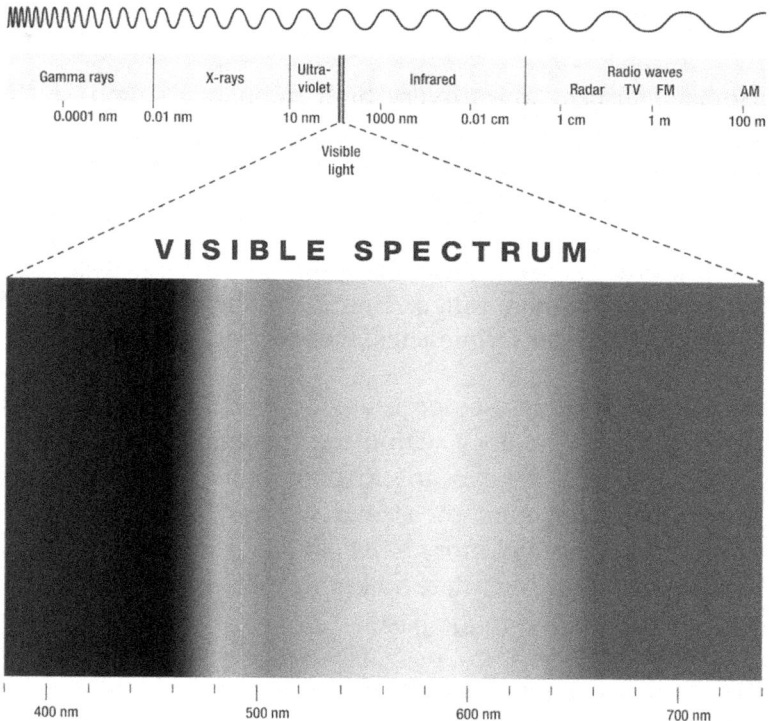

So in essence, different species are experiencing different worlds, they see different worlds, they see the world differently. Other species may see and hear and experience events in their reality that we humans do not and cannot.

For example, A dog's sense of smell is said to be a one to ten thousand times more sensitive than that of humans. In fact, a dog can have more than 220 million olfactory receptors in its nose, depending on the breed, while humans have only 5 million.[6]

Horses can hear low to very high frequency sound, in the range of 14 Hz to 25 kHz (human range is generally 20 Hz to 20 kHz). Studies have shown horses to hear each other up to 4400 meters away which is just under 3 miles.[7]

Several animal species are able to hear frequencies well beyond the human range. Some dolphins and bats, for example, can hear frequencies in excess of 100 Khz.[8]

These other species see or sense the world differently. Just as each one of us does within our extended global human family. When we have an expanded sense of vision, our world looks different to us and we are experiencing life from a different and more expansive and inclusive vantage point. We see things that others cannot, or that we could not and did not see in the past.

What we experience as vision through our eyes works in this way. Here is our understanding of vision up through present day, courtesy of the *American Optometric Association*...

"How Your Eyes Work"

"Vision begins when light rays are reflected off an object and enter the eyes through the cornea, the transparent outer covering of the eye. The cornea bends or refracts the rays that pass through a round hole called the pupil. The iris, or colored portion of the eye that surrounds the pupil, opens and closes (making the pupil bigger or smaller) to regulate the amount of light passing through. The light rays then pass through the lens, which actually changes shape so it can further bend the rays and focus them on the retina at the back of the eye. The retina is a thin layer of tissue at the back of the eye that contains millions of tiny light-sensing nerve cells called rods and cones, which are named for their distinct shapes. Cones are concentrated in the center of the retina, in an area called the macula. In bright light conditions, cones provide clear, sharp central vision and detect colors and fine details. Rods are located outside the macula and extend all the way to the outer edge of the retina. They provide peripheral or side vision. Rods also allow the eyes to detect motion and help us see in dim light and at night. These cells in the retina convert the light into electrical impulses. The optic nerve sends these impulses to the brain where an image is produced."[9]

In other words, our eyes and brain work together to translate images.

But where do the images originate from? Are they out there or are they expected, in our minds, and then we see them out there? Are there an infinite number of possibilities to be seen? Is there a spectrum that we "see" on which we experience our lives individually, based on our prior patterns?

In essence our minds, our brains, the wonderful supercomputers that they are, are translating vibrational waves, information, into something that appears as real to us in the outside world. Seemingly tangible things that we can also decode and enjoy (or not) with our other senses also of touch, hearing, smell, and if appropriate taste. We would enjoy a fine meal and a book in a different manner, of course, with appropriate senses. All of our senses work in a similar way for a certain end in that they are each a different way of translating frequency or vibration.

Vision Development

It is interesting to note how we as a species develop our sense of vision. According to the *American Optometric Association*, "Vision, and how the brain uses visual information, are learned skills." The AOA notes, "Babies learn to see over a period of time, much like they learn to walk and talk. They are not born with all the visual abilities they need in life. The ability to focus their eyes, move them accurately, and use them together as a team must be learned. Also, they need to learn how to use the visual information the eyes send to their brain in order to understand the world around them and interact with it appropriately."[10]

Your brain and eyes work together to translate your world. Basically your ability to see in this reality is learned.

In every way.

I'll repeat this because this is an important point I'd like to convey...

Basically, your ability to see in this reality is learned.

In every way.

Interestingly, from birth to about three months of age, the focus of an infant's eyes is limited to 8 to 10 inches from their face. As they grow they begin to see farther and in more developed ways. An infant's world is all about them, as any parent knows, and this is the vision field or range or vicinity that they need to begin life here. Their parents will be close by to tend to them in their world, to lovingly meet their needs. Babies are great communicators too to assist us in meeting their needs.

I would posit that:

> *Your ability to see in this reality is learned.*
> *In every way.*
>
> *... We learned how to see physically with our eyes. And we learned the way we see the world, our world, from the opinions that we learned from others.*

As we grow, our world expands. And as you continue to evolve further into the true visionary that you were always meant to be, your vision will expand to ever greater levels too.

We are taught about the world, how the world works from our parents, caregivers and society during our time here. Just as a baby physically learns to see the world, we learn to mentally see the world.

We learn to see not only in an actual physical sense as babies learning to use our eyes and eye/brain system to see images. We also learn to see various situations, memes, beliefs, and thoughts about the world from our parents, family, society and community into which we are born. For example, an older child may have a different vision of his world than the youngest child of the family. A child born into a family in a small rural town in Europe may have a different point of view than a person born in NYC or Tokyo; and likewise, a person born in a remote village in Africa will see life differently too.

Once we understand that we literally and figuratively learn how to see, we can understand more clearly choices that we make and have made, habits that we have perpetuated, and our current worldview. We learn how to see as part of our human physical development. What we learn is impressed upon us from our surroundings. And we learn _what_ we see, what our world is and the impressions or feelings around those images. And, in turn, we learn what _to_ see. By our expectations (and more importantly and first before ours, others' expectations, when we are babies and young children) and our surroundings. Here is the T-H-B-P again, passed on to us from our setting. Therefore, you can now understand how our ability to see in this reality is learned. The extent to which we can see is governed by our environment's impressions upon us, expansive or restrictive. We see what our parents and society expect and have learned to see in their worlds.

We look out there and "see" the world, right?

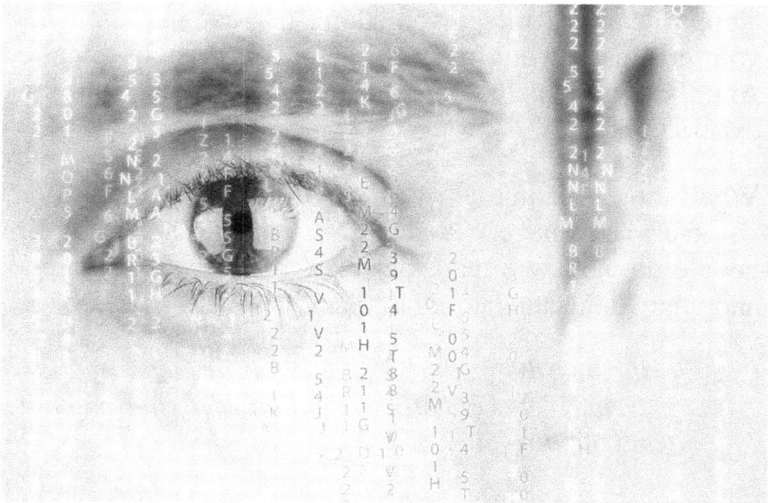

This is reality after all, correct? This is what we have been taught, what conventional wisdom has impressed upon us.

But What If...

Vision actually works in a different way than we were taught. We are taught that there are objects and images "out there" that we can translate with our eyes and brain to "see" and experience. And these objects and images are limited and fixed. Everybody sees the same thing in this reality when you look in a particular direction or at a particular subject.

But what about seeing in your mind's eye, dreaming, or people who are considered blind. None of these scenarios involve input from the eyes. That is, it is not required to "look out there" to see something in your mind's eye, in your dreams, in your imagination, or for the sight-impaired. And these may include the most detailed visions and vivid experiences.

What about visionaries who see things that others don't yet see. They have a vision for a creation, that at first people thought was mad, but then after it was envisioned and created, became commonplace.

> *Humans flying though the air in a metal cylinder? "Crazy!" ...Until the invention of flying machines and the airplane.*

Rockets outside of our atmosphere? "Science fiction," said the people of the 1800s.

Said to Thomas Edison, "You mean this round looking object can provide light?" Now I <u>know</u> you must be insane.

What if...

What if what we see in our mind's eye... we then have the potential ability to see with our physical eyes, our eye/brain system of seeing.

What if...

We create the images in our mind and then project them out into the world, "seeing them", making them visible, making them reality. We project our symbolic reality. We create in our minds what we would like to see. And then we "find" these things out there in the world that we call our reality. They are in our visible spectrum of reality. The waves of information that we have allowed ourselves access to. When we grow and evolve, we see more. We expand our vision. We see things that we did not see before. Our world becomes different, improved, more of what we want to see, what lies in the seeds of our desires for our lives.

I would posit that: We create our worlds and then see them into being. We are seeing ourselves. Reflected out there.

And… We have developed patterns of "seeing". We can re-*learn* or re-*create* the way that we see the world, thus changing our experience of the world. Thus changing our world. Thus creating our world.

We'll discuss the how-to's of this in a moment…. But first let's get some basics down as a foundation.

> *We create our worlds and then see them into being.*
> *We are seeing ourselves. Reflected out there.*

And... We have developed patterns of "seeing". We can re-learn or re-create the way that we see the world, thus changing our experience of the world. Thus, changing our world. Thus creating our world.

Humans as Projectors. Eyes of God

Cue the projector, roll the film...

After our impressionable youth, our growing years as babies and children, we enter our adolescent and teenage years. We, still in that phase as *Recorders*, record but begin to realize a greater sense of self. We begin to question the world and authority. Ask any parent with children of teenage years! We begin to assert our own independence. We are at that transitional stage between Recorders and Projectors.

We've discussed that from birth and into young infancy, an infant sees the world as himself. He cannot distinguish yet between where he ends and the world begins. He needs to "learn" this as part of his development.

We then progress as babies and children to record our impressions of the world that we were born into, our surroundings. We read-write as we are in the Recorder stage.

As we progress into the teenage years we as human beings take our development to the next level and begin to see

43

ourselves more as autonomous beings. We are usually given more responsibilities and can see the results of our actions and choices. This helps to prepare us later on as we grow into adulthood.

As we enter adulthood and move out on our own we take full responsibility for our choices and are allowed and encouraged by society to test our wings. It is that special time.

Like a caterpillar into a butterfly, an entirely different creature from that which it began, we also go through a transformation. In our human technological development we have changed from *Recorders* to *Projectors*.

As a Projector, we project our world out there as we think it is, sometimes as we think it ought to be, but always as a projection at this point from our programming from the Recorder stage of our development.

What we see, we are inside. Those patterns, standing wave emanations of thought, belief, and habit. We see the world as it has been taught to us, as it has been impressed upon us, in our RAM, random access memory.

If we have been taught:

- That the world is a bad place, bad things "happen", we may likely experience the unwanted.

- That the world is cold-hearted and mean, we may likely continue to experience cold relationships. In part because that is what we expect, and in part because that may be what we are offering. Either we are cold as a protective measure, or we get what we expect and continue to feel hurt.

- That the world is scarce in resources, then we will experience scarcity.

- That the world is abundant, then we will experience abundance. We will create abundance.

- That the world is loving. Then we will experience a loving world. Because we are loving. Because we are love.

And this last one above is a universal truth, a hidden secret of the universe, that, sadly, not all of us are able to "see" and experience. We *are* love, all of us. Each one of us. All the Eyes of God. It's just that some of us had a lapse in memory of this truth during what was impressed upon us during the Recorder stage.

But everyone will find their way back to this truth, sooner or later, one way or another. Let's find out how....

Projection

We <u>see</u> the world as we <u>are</u>.

What you see in the outside world is a reflection of your inside world. It is a projection.

But what is "out there"? Since we are Projectors - we are projecting our insides out. The world looks to us as we are. The world can be beautiful. Or the world can be a frightening and fearful place. The world can appear to be a prison; although we are actually imprisoning ourselves never realizing we have the key and the cell is open. Or the world, our world, can be a loving, scintillating, joyful, place... when we become more of who we *really* are.

We are individual projectors in a collective reality, all having different experiences. We each can experience the same event, person, place or thing very differently.

This is actually an ingenious technology. If you don't like what you see, then change what is inside. Then you will project an entirely different world. You will see different outcomes and have different experiences if you so choose.

So, what you "see" out there - is really you. Facets of you, reflecting back to you. And, even if you can't see it yet, it is indescribably brilliant and beautiful. Because that is who YOU are at your essence, at your core. You may just need to tweak the programming a little to your liking or change the program entirely. The program was given to you, it did not originate from you. It is now your choice to upgrade your software, if you so choose. Perhaps those around you in your youth, when you were in the Recorder stage, couldn't reflect all of the beauty that is you, and this resulted in cloudy vision for you now. A cloudy projection, a mere shadow of who you really are.

Perhaps at times, or even for long stretches of time, you experienced yourself and life from the shadows, the shadows of your being. Please know that these are not your shadows. They are mere distortions on the way that you were seen, thus now how you "see". You can change this.

> *It is no coincidence that the word "vision" describes both the way you see in the world (eyesight) and what you project in the world (your vision).*

Projection in Relationships

> *Relationships between two people are intersections of worlds. They are gifts to us. It is like expanded*

vision, seeing with two sets of eyes, two perspectives, two vantage points. Each person has their blind spots. Each person has a field of vision. Two people, two points.

Relationships in our world are often formed in the mind, played in the mind, and sometimes destroyed from the mind. We project our fantasies and preferences onto another. We project our inner fears and discord onto another. Our projections sometimes consist of what we want in another person, conditions placed by us, often subconsciously, on how we think they should act, how they should be, express and feel. This is not necessarily a recipe for ease and honoring. It is however a recipe for our learning and continued growth. We can get to see what our beliefs and patterns are via these projections and reflections.

Relationships are the delicious way that we learn about ourselves and find our inner divine love, find out who we are, what we are made of, what is important to us, even why we are here. Not to mention that they can be a source of joy, fun, and part of our greatest happiness. But, to gain the most, to "see" the most, we must learn to embrace the full spectrum of all that they are which can represent our greatest joys as well as our greatest sorrows. Relationships are full spectrum just as life is, just as the world is. We cannot grow and love more fully from our hearts, open our hearts, until we integrate what appears to be light and dark, good and bad. Without the contrast of the lows we would not know our preferences or feel the highs.

We project our love and our fears.

We project our fears of intimacy, opening our hearts only as fully as we are capable, by pushing the other away through actions or inaction.

We project our fear of rejection by rejecting the other before they can reject us.

We project our own insecurities through jealousy and accusation and sometimes the imposition of a sort of imprisonment.

We project our inadequate self-reliance and care of self by feeling that someone or something "owes" us in the way of money or of doting solely on us.

We project our own unhappiness and cowardice by putting down or hurting those who have the audacity to be happy and to express their true spirit.

We project our inability to allow ourselves to actually "see" ourselves and others and to open our hearts.

These are all scenarios that give your power away to something outside of yourself. The gift in this is the realization that it is not the other person's issues that are making us miserable, it is we projecting some programming onto them, producing either the Pygmalion Effect or the

Golem Effect. When we realize that there is a better and more joyful way, then we will stop blaming and start honoring. When we honor ourselves, then we must honor the other. Because the other is a representation, a projection of our own inner thoughts, what we think of the world.

Love yourself, then enjoy more fully a relationship with another. Fill yourself up. You can't give from an empty cup.

Let your vessel, your chalice, runneth over with love, respect and honor. Then drink deeply and share the joy within.

The Blame Game

So am I to blame if my life isn't going my way?

No, of course not.

Blame and guilt are only projections of you believing erroneously that you are not intelligent enough nor worthy enough to actually be the creator of your life. To see through the Eyes of God that you have been given.

If things have not been going your way, it is because you are only acting and making choices from your old Thoughts-Habits-Beliefs-Patterns, consciously or behind the scenes. And these old T-H-B-P you picked up in your Recorder phase and along your journey.

And you can make a choice at any time to look in a new direction, toward your dreams, toward what makes you feel the best, toward what you really want in life.

So are others to blame if my life isn't going my way?

Like my parents, who provided me with the software when I grew up, or an ex-spouse, or the people in my life now or others whom I have had experiences with?

No, of course not. Your parents lovingly were the best parents that they could be, that they knew how to be. So was your ex-spouse. Same with that annoying neighbor or that critical person at work.

If they could behave in a different way, *then they would.* But they are emanating who they are inside, that is, the standing wave of the patterns that they recorded. Who they have learned to be.

This does not make them bad.

We assign "good" or "bad" to how something makes us feel. <u>We</u> give life meaning.

Your parent not driving you to the ballgame when you were ten years old may have been given a "bad" label by you. But, who knows, maybe there was a terrible accident on that road that, had you gone there, you would have been injured or worse. Divine guidance. .. Or they may have lost their job if they took one more afternoon off, causing the family to eventually not be able to put food on the table or lose your home.

You don't know... what you don't know. And you can't see... what you can't see.

Until...

You expand your vision.

And when you do this, situations, people, places and things always look different. They always look different when you have more information, a wider perspective, and more wisdom.

And this happens, when you look with added depth and presence with how you are actually supposed to see, with and through your Eyes of God, rather than through the limited vision that you had perhaps allowed yourself before.

Why do bad things happen to good people?

A 10-year-old boy looks out on the smoky battlefield called his city. His father and brother had been taken away as carnage over the past year in the war in his bloody and battered city, his place of birth. He is now left to care for his mother and two younger sisters. With no money and an uncertain future, today is questionable. How they will live. If they will live.

He cries out to the smoky sky, "Why is the world like this? Why does this have to happen?

Why was I born? And born here. Why would I choose this?"

Eyes of God?

Yes, I say. Absolutely.

We are all born at a particular place in time. We cannot do anything about the world that we arrived into prior to our being here. It is what it is and all that it has become. In its heaven or hellish state depending on where you stand or where you land. Where you begin.

How on earth or in heaven can this be?

We are born into a particular place or family or situation… to read-write and record what we see. It is not our task to wallow in self-pity. It is not our task to be doomed to a lifetime of oppression, depression, or despair. It is however wholly our task to take where we are at, what we see, and to transform that into something that is much better. And to use our Eyes of God to create a better place. Something that is much more pleasant to look at, to experience, to live.

> *It is our work here to take where we are at, what we see, and transform that into something that is much better. And to use our Eyes of God to create a better place. Something that is much more pleasant to look at, to experience, to live.*

Compassion and Pity

Compassion is casting a loving gaze at those who you would like to assist, your brothers and sisters of our human family. Compassion feels good to those involved. It's intention is based in love, understanding, and support.

Pity, though, is a misunderstanding of a situation. It is not seeing through your full Eyes of God. It feels bad to the person looking and to the person being looked at in pity. If you expanded your vision, you would see the beauty in what you were looking at, the beauty of the essence of a person, helping them to feel strong and instilling the knowing that they can overcome whatever their situation may be. Having pity on someone is offering disempowerment toward them. It does not help you or the person. In fact, it creates an opportunity for disempowerment for them. Pity is from your perspective, not theirs. They may be just fine! They may have different values than you.

If you look in the direction of someone and actually see them in all of their glory, then you can help them. Sure, they may be going through a difficult time, or may have made some not so healthful choices, but who they are at their core, is the essence of God, just like you.

They are no different from you. It's just that they may have been born at a particular point, a focus, a locus, where they didn't experience life as sweet in their Recorder stage. And they haven't figured out yet how to alchemize that experience

> *We cause evolution to happen. As the Eyes of God, we create and project situations where we all grow. And everyone benefits. Including who or what is behind our eyes.*

We sometimes think that creation is merely only creation of more humans, procreation. But creation happens every day. It's all around us. You see, we are the human creators, the Eyes of God. The representations here on this earth in human form to cast our vision in the direction of a more loving, enlightened, and beautiful experience for all here. And by all here I mean not just humans, I'm talking about everything that we see, all beings, all matter. For everything that we see is the creation, it is spiritual matter, Spirit in matter, matter in spirit.

Everything matters! It's spiritual matter!

What about the people perpetuating the war and turmoil in the boy's city? Are they Eyes of God too?

Some of us have lost our way in the story and we cannot see clearly a path to a better way; our vision is obscured and we cannot see the glory that is meant to be. Perhaps they were born into the same city, with the same old battles, with the same despair. They have not yet seen their real reason for being there. Like the little 10-year-old boy who will discover his purpose, his true life calling. Maybe he will be the next Gandhi, Abraham Lincoln, Martin Luther King, Jr. or Nelson Mandela. A leader who will bring people out of war, out of oppression and into a better experience, the promised land.

It is never too late for the the other characters, the older people in the boy's story, who are waging the battles. It is never too late for anyone to discover their true purpose, their inner essence, which is always love. All it takes to begin is turning in the direction of what feels best, a better experience, a better world.

Turn to look in the direction of what feels best. This is the direction of the promised land. You know the way by how you feel.

Interestingly, we think that our children are provided to us to carry on our traditions, our standing belief wave patterns, our old ways of thinking and being. Sometimes we even try to force them into these ways.

In actuality they are here to lovingly move all of us and our family lines forward to a new level of creation that's even better. Made up of all the best parts of the past and all the wondrous parts of things to come.

Appreciate the past. Love the present. Create the future.

If we attempt to keep our progeny only steeped in the past then we take away the opportunity for their gifts to us, their gifts to themselves, and their gifts to the world. Our children are here to provide us, all of us, with a new view, a new angle on the world. A new set of Eyes of God. To see you from a new vantage point. And you as parents have miraculously brought them here and made this possible to do that. *Thank you!*

As we approach adulthood, we, steeped in our T-H-B-P from our Recorder years, usually enter into significant relationships or partner relationships with others. These can provide a wealth of joy and growth for both parties involved.

Our relationships are treasures. Projections, reflections and love. Borne from love.

You can only ever change a situation with love.
You can never change a situation with hate.

You can't hate something into change.
You can only love something into change.
Love changes everything.

Hate changes nothing. It keeps you at a particular point on a line, going further and further downward, sinking into a hellish quagmire.

But love… love moves you forward. And upward. And anywhere that you want to go.

Levels of Relationship

How relationships sometimes work... *before you realize who you really are.*

You want something, for example, love. Instead of going inside and being it, you look for it outside. It must be somewhere ...This often results in a situation where, instead of projecting love and receiving that same high level of love, you look for it in another to give to you. It does not work like this and this only sets you up for immediate or eventual disappointment. But in order to avoid years of struggle and heartache, instead, you can learn to become the thing itself. It is a human energetic physics that you will attract a resonant energy or vibration. If you cannot be love inside of yourself, then you will not attract the love that you so crave. If you can only open your heart so much, then that small opening will determine the amount of love that will be reflected back to you.

Reflection also works in more joyous ways too. When we are fully present in the moment such as with our children or our beloved or with our creative work, we channel out and receive back the maximum joyous essence of our interactions. When we have learned to be still with our mental mind chatter not getting in the way of our hearts' desires then magic happens. Doors open that we didn't "see" before. When we are at peace with ourselves then we can be at peace with others. And with any situation that may arise. When you are centered then this is possible. When you do not look "out there" to change the world around you, but instead look inside and change the world inside you as you would like your outer world to be, then success can be speedy.

You would not want another stating to you that, "You need to behave in this or that particular way for me to be happy." or "You need to pay attention to my needs before yours." or "If you don't do this then I won't love you anymore." These are all conditional ways of loving another, restricting and constricting your vision and robbing you and them of the truly delicious experience that you could be having. This restricted vision is certainly not befitting of the beloved. And the beloved is actually... *you*. The fact is that what we give out is reflected back to us. When you can exude love, as unconditional as you can in this game that we call life, then you will resonate with those who are the same high level frequency who can actually love you back in the way that you want, the way and to the degree that you have learned to love yourself.

And, applying the Pygmalion Effect, if you know that your relationship is capable of being even better than it is at current, and this is always the case - remember why you came together in the first place, the feelings that you felt, then give that unconditional love. And see what happens. Remember what you love about your partner. Remember what you love about life, about yourself. Remember that you... are love.

If you believe yourself worthy of love, honor and respect, then that is what will be reflected back to you in your world. Those that do not match this will tend to move out of your experience and be replaced with something that does match your evolving and loving self.

What is Love, Anyway?

What is love? What is falling in love?

Being in love is the striking act of recognizing yourself in another, the best parts of yourself, from a higher vantage point. From your higher vantage point, Eyes of God, looking down through you, to you, and at you. It is projecting outside of you the love that you are inside. It is finding an other as a clear screen for your personal prism of love's expression, what is beautiful and important to you, in your heart. And shining that beauty onto another. And they are doing the same with you. It is using your Eyes of God to create a heaven on earth within the chalice of a relationship. And the other, the beloved's, Eyes of God are focused on you with the same pure gaze.

How beautiful and delicious is that!

How do you keep the feeling of being in love?

When two people are in love with one another, if you have ever had this fortunate and unmistakable experience, it feels like walking in heaven, time suspended, your heart is open, you are inspired to great heights of emotion, feeling, and brilliance.

It is only when one or both falls out of heaven that the feeling goes away.

Your vision becomes clouded, you see less than. T-H-B-P creeps in. Your metaphorical depth perception greatly decreases. Rather than experiencing brilliant colors you see shades of gray. Or darkness.

Love need not be fleeting.

Because it is a state of being. It is not "out there". It is inside. Projected through and out.

If you desire a soul-stirring, wholehearted, delicious love affair relationship with your partner, you can stay in love, in heaven, with your partner. To stay in heaven, you do this… by *being* love. By being your true authentic self, which is love, exuding love, and this is a most amazing experience for anyone in your presence. Best of all, for yourself. Your partner, after all, is a reflection of your beliefs about yourself, love, relationship, your worth, your worthiness, and your inner world.

The secret of this all is to be in love. Meaning you, yourself, are love. You emanate love and live love. You are *in* love, standing inside of love. When you are a point as such mainly then everything that you look at in your world will be through loving eyes. And those that match your love will reflect back to you the beauty of this world. Creating new levels of heaven with them.

Success

What does success mean to you? Is it about becoming super-rich? About experiences? About family? Your children? About your career? Your business? Having leisure time?

We all have different ideas of what we want our outer world to look like and what is important to us personally. When we see with expanded vision, it grows those areas of our lives that we wish to focus upon, those areas that are important to us.

A Love Story, a Drama and a Comedy

> *All the world's a stage, And all the men and women merely players.*
> *From William Shakespeare's As You Like It*

The world is akin to a live theatre production or a movie. Or an interactive video or online game. And we are merely players....

You as avatar.

Our thoughts project what our brain/eyes see, what we see. We translate signals and vibrational waves and then we see our interpretation of what the world is. Our view. Our world view.

> *Sure, we started out in our parent's/city's/country/ society/generation's view of the game. But it is entirely up to us which game we choose to play in the future. And the future always starts now. How could you improve upon life as you know it? This is why you are here.*

How this works is in this way. If we are basically projectors, and project our world, the world that we see, we can be certain that every other individual projector on the planet is doing the same thing. They are looking at life from their own beliefs (that have been taught to them), their own prejudices, their own fears, their own hopes, their own learned behaviors. Much like a computer, our bodies are the hardware with our brain as the CPU, and the program (Thought-Habit-Belief-Pattern, T-H-B-P) is our software. And we all have a unique program. It was coded as we were growing up. It was coded by the experiences we had, and even these were based on the coded experiences of others. So you are carrying a multi-generational upgraded, somewhat newer version but old software program.

However, as an adult Projector, you have the power within you to change your entire environment, your outside energetic milieu, your standing wave emanation, by changing your inside energetic milieu, your standing wave emanation, your T-H-B-P.

The resulting projections thus are evolved and changed. And you don't need scientific studies with varying statistical data including, in part, the observer effect to prove this. Just look around. You can see that each newer generation brings in new ideas, gets more progressive, lives longer, creates new themes and memes that build upon and add to the previous.

But this cannot happen fully, easily, or expeditiously if you do not shine your brilliance, who you really are, your unique inner gifts. The fact is, you create your experience and improve upon that informational software as you go along. Because you *are* the Eyes of God.

Our Visual Acuity

We use our eye/brain system to see and project our world.

If we are really Eyes of God, then does "how we see" or "how well we see" have an effect on "what we see"? Is there a metaphorical correlation?

Let's take a look at our eye/brain system next, which allows us to see the world, or rather interpret it in a visual way. Let's explore....

Perfect Vision

What is perfect vision? Is it the 20/20 designation that the ophthalmologist or optometrist pronounces after a standardized test? I think that perfect vision is the ability to love what we see. To out-picture in the world from the highest evolved point of our being at any point in time. To "see" heaven on earth. That is… to create heaven on earth. Because what we "see" is what is inside.

With that said, our physical vision can sometimes be a reflection of our internal vision. I feel that there is a metaphorical correlation. Vision with our eyes often and can be a reflection on our internal mechanics of sight. So, the better you see, the more clear your world appears. And is.

Let's take a metaphorical journey… shall we?

Vision Issues and Distortions

Nearsightedness

"Nearsightedness, or Myopia, as it is medically termed, is a vision condition in which close objects are seen clearly, but objects farther away appear blurred. Nearsightedness occurs if the eyeball is too long or the cornea, the clear front cover of the eye, has too much curvature. As a result, the light entering the eye isn't focused correctly and distant objects look blurred.

Nearsightedness is a very common vision condition affecting nearly 30 percent of the US population. Some research supports the theory that nearsightedness is hereditary. There is also growing evidence that it is influenced by the visual stress of too much close work."[11]

We have all experienced nearsightedness in our vision of life. Sometimes we look so closely we don't see the bigger picture. Sometimes people "can't see the forest for the trees". They can see what is immediate but not the impact of their actions in the larger picture. These people are generally great at close up details. That is a talent of the nearsighted. But the larger picture, more difficult to see for the nearsighted. Were they born with nearsighted vision? Did it develop in childhood or adulthood?

The metaphorical nearsighted or shortsighted can learn to expand their vision if they so desire. To look further "out there" to see a larger picture. Doing so may help them fit together pieces of their lives that did not make sense in the past. For it is a new way of looking at things. It is an expanded way, an expanded view. It is a stretch. Just as we stretch our hamstring muscles to train for a run or stretch other muscles in yoga or Pilates, we can stretch our literal and metaphoric vision muscles. [12]

When we stretch our figurative vision muscles, we can see things in a new way, in an expanded way, see a larger world, our expanded world. With all of the expanded opportunities, fun and delight that may exist. That we have been missing all this time. As with stretching our muscles, yoga/stretching for our eyesight, or yoga/stretching for our vision, expands us in new ways so we can have a wider range of vision. *(See www.LindaLaFlamme.com for additional information.)* Not stuck in rigid patterns and only being able to focus from learned habit on a certain comfort range of near or far, but both equally well and perhaps even with more acuity and clarity at a closer distance as well as farther, makes for balanced vision.

I had a period of time in my own life of literal decreased vision. When I was going to university for my graduate degree, (while also running a business, traveling each week, maintaining a long distance relationship, and more), I realized that I was having trouble seeing the board in class in the lecture hall. My vision was not in its usual top form. I developed a need for glasses due to a case of "nearsightedness", which I believe was self-imposed. Fortunately, when we realize that something is self-imposed, we can later make it self-corrective.

In my reality at the time in grad school, I was not allowing myself to look at the bigger picture of my life. I was only focused on getting through the now, getting through each semester, getting through the day, each exhausting day.

Not paying attention to the sacrifices, lack of free time, rigid schedule, decreased self-care due to my ridiculous and self-imposed schedule, my vision of life became consumed with immediate tasks and projects. I was focused on my immediate needs of getting through each day. Even my partner at the time was long-distance and I couldn't see him as often as I wanted. I am smiling as I type these words because this seems so crazy and yet so obvious to me now. But not then. Because my vision was cloudy. It was distorted for that period of time. I had forgotten my long-term happiness and larger picture of health to focus specifically on the moment, for survival really, to get through my degree. I developed other effects too of my self-imposed schedule and eventually a condition of Chronic Fatigue.

But as I completed grad school, I made changes in my life, healed from CFS, and then my vision was restored back to great. When I healed I didn't need glasses anymore. Although I was grateful for them during the time they assisted me.

My glasses allowed me to keep my patterns, or rather to be functional in the patterns I had set for myself. And still see. I am very thankful that I had the option to have glasses. But I am also thankful that I learned to look at the bigger picture of my life and to make changes. And I am thankful that my vision "returned to my normal" after that. Actually, it was improved.

Farsightedness

"Farsightedness, or Hyperopia, as it is medically termed, is a vision condition in which distant objects are usually seen clearly, but close ones do not come into proper focus. Farsightedness occurs if your eyeball is too short or the cornea has too little curvature, so light entering your eye is not focused correctly.

Common signs of farsightedness include difficulty in concentrating and maintaining a clear focus on near objects, eye strain, fatigue and/or headaches after close work, aching or burning eyes, irritability or nervousness after sustained concentration."[13]

My beautiful mother, who transitioned out of her life when I was a teenager, was farsighted. That is, she needed glasses to see up close. From my perspective, respectfully, she could not and did not want to see many things that were right in front of her, literally and figuratively. I noticed that she was great in looking at issues at a distance, but was not quite as good at tending to issues that were very close to home. She was taught to look "out there" for life, not at herself, her wants, her needs, or her desires. She believed that extreme self-sacrifice was virtuous, her self-worth was low, and she ignored her body's health needs. She never learned to see differently than that pattern. Everything else out there in the distance was more important to her than what was up close and personal. She would joke, although it was not funny, that she took better care of her car than herself. Maybe it was a cry for help. A cry for acknowledgement that attention to herself and her needs was just as important as anything "out there". She knew this somewhere deep in her soul but her habits and beliefs kept her in the same patterns.

Where are you farsighted in life? Are you missing out on important and joyous things that are very close to you? Your family? Your own happiness? Is there something that you don't want to see? Is there an elephant in the room?

The thing with those elephants is, that once you actually take a look at them squarely, you can make choices to improve the situation, to enhance your life. Then they're not an elephant in the room anymore. They were a mountain but now they look more like a molehill, not as foreboding and shadowy.

Whenever you shine a light onto something, the object becomes less "shadowy" and more manageable. You know what you are looking at, or at least have a better idea than before.

> *Sometimes people focus so much "out there" and in the distance that they forget what is important to them, to their soul. It is in combining the best aspects of all depths of vision that we can live a full and joyous life.*

Colorblindness

Isn't it grand to see in as many colors as possible? Many variations, hues, shades, nuances of color. This makes life rich, textural, and filled with brilliance.

A life of just black and white can get boring. This way or that way. This or that, good or bad, right or wrong. My way or the highway. But a life of color, a full spectrum of beautiful, bursting color, this is why we are here.

The more different hues, shades and variations that we can see, distinguish, honor and love, the more expansive our vision palette will be.

These hues may take the shape of the next steps on your journey, wading into the refreshing water rather than dipping your toe in. Different shades and variations may include exploring your inner passions and raison d'être. It may include expanding your repertoire of trying new activities, foods, friends, visiting new places, learning new skills and developing previously hidden talents. And it may, just may, include experiencing deeper levels of love. Deeper levels of yourself.

> *Dive in to these beautiful colors and vibrant experiences. Live your life in full color.*

When you are able to see and to embrace the full spectrum of color, you live a life of visual texture and richness. This is why the appearance of a rainbow in the sky is visually appealing to us. It includes a visible spectrum of color, not just one tone. Not sepia. But it represents our true nature, a reflection of many glorious colors.

Clarity

…In addition to seeing in full color, we also want to see as clearly as we can. Blurred vision is a condition that many have. As we have been discussing, curiously, our physical eyesight conditions can sometimes provide us with clues to improve our vision in general.

As above, so below.

Blurred Vision

Blurred vision occurs with almost everyone to varying degrees at some point. Who hasn't experienced blurred vision at least at some point in their lives?

According to the AOA, "Astigmatism is a vision condition that causes blurred vision due either to the irregular shape of the cornea, the clear front cover of the eye, or sometimes the curvature of the lens inside the eye".... "Astigmatism is a very common vision condition. Most people have some degree of astigmatism. Slight amounts of astigmatism usually don't affect vision and don't require treatment. However, larger amounts cause distorted or blurred vision, eye discomfort and headaches."[14]

If the aspiration is to be your best visionary self, as clear as possible Eyes of God, then you will want to clear up your vision as best you can. In a figurative sense. To attain the happiness and success that is your birthright, you must desire and be willing to look at your life, and life in general, from varying depths, and with increasing clarity and acuity. This is the first step on the visionary path. On the creative path. Of creating the life that you were really meant to live. Of creating the world around you that is a heaven on earth.

If you cannot see yourself clearly then it is difficult to articulate the highest vision for your life. There is a correlation between how you see yourself and how you see your world. The degree of increasing clarity from which you see the world reflects your expanded influence, potency, and the impact that you have on the world that you see. It all starts with you. Everything starts with you.

Depth Perception

A person of depth and character is a welcome companion. The more depth you can see, the greater degree of profundity you can experience in your life, and the deeper the levels of human connection, people, places and things you can experience with profound richness, flavor and substance.

When we have a shallow view of the world, it appears quite uninteresting. We see the surface but miss out on the 20,000 leagues under the sea. We see a person's face but do not see into their soul. Into their heart, into their dreams. Into their Eyes of God.

The greater the degree you can increase your depth perception within your life, the more texture and meaning you can experience. From what is in front of you, right here and right now. With your loved ones, with your children, with your surroundings. With everything.

How to increase depth perception with your physical eyesight?

Ophthalmologists may tell you to focus your gaze at close objects, for repeated intervals throughout the day, then focus off in the distance, then bring your focus to the mid-point of that. At each point allowing your eyes to adjust to see with more clarity each point of varying depths. This keeps your physical depth perception vision strong and acute with an expanded range. If we focus or look only at a specific distance all of the time, say our computer screen, or only way off in the distance, then our eyes become accustomed to that particular defined spectrum range of view.

How to increase your metaphorical depth perception?

You can play a fun game with yourself about expanding your vision, in this case your depth perception. Challenge yourself to see something from a different angle - about your partner or spouse, about your work, about your children. Go a little deeper on a topic that you'd like to explore. Ask someone else's perspective on an issue. See the why's behind the situations. Look at the motivations of others behind the actions. All are valid, most are borne from T-H-B-P, and all are unique and interesting. This expands your depth perception muscles and allows your experience to become a little bit richer each time you do this.

The more angles from which we can see, the more points (of view) that we can understand, the greater wisdom we gain. Then our vision expands, our worldview grows, and the canvas of our lives grows and becomes richer to explore and to enjoy and to continue evolving from forward.

Vision and Age

Curiously our vision often changes as we age. Just as a baby can see only under 12 inches up to a few months of age, sometimes when we approach our 40's or 50's our vision focus range is farther, we may become farsighted. Maybe we have a tendency to look more at our impact on the world at that point in our lives? The children may have grown and moved out, we may be looking further outside, and not immediately in front of us so much as we did, as was required, before.

In my research I found that "Farsightedness often runs in families." I found this interesting. The research also noted, "Farsightedness often starts in early childhood. But normal growth corrects the problem."[15] This is interesting and somewhat telling. All a part of growing up.

Substances and Vision

Blurry vision can result when we imbibe and overdo it with external substances, overloading our systems. A side effect, or more correctly an effect, of indulging in mind-altering drugs such as overuse or abuse of alcohol or other substances is distorted vision while we are under the influence. Our "focus" is temporarily taken off of our lives while we are ingesting the substances.

In my dark years as a teen after my family died, I longed for something that would dull the pain. I dabbled in alcohol for a short period of time before I realized that it was causing more pain for an even worse experience.

Substances can dull our pain or help us to not see something painful for the moment, providing a short respite of relief. But this is an ineffective way of treating the symptoms (painful situations) and not treating the root issues (projection of erroneous learned patterns). Mind (vision) altering substances can make the pain seem to temporarily disappear, because they dull our vision, along with many other things, but they're not the solution.

The solution is to image the world we prefer in our minds and hearts and then project it out into the world so that we (and others too) can experience it.

So, I would postulate again that the way that some people see with their physical eyes may, in some cases, have a figurative correlation to their inner world view. Their inner way of seeing. Their habits, patterns and proclivities.

I say *many people* because there are groups of us, other Eyes of God, who "see" in a different way.

Different Ways of Seeing

The Different Way of Interpreting That We Call Blindness

What about those who cannot see in the traditional sense, those who are considered blind or legally blind by our modern standards? Well, they can see, but just not in the way that most people see.

If the images are nerve impulses translated by the brain, then the person receives a translation, just a different one that sighted humans do.

In fact, some people who cannot or could not "see" in the traditional eye translation sense, have or had great vision. Take Helen Keller for example. Or take the musical genius of Stevie Wonder. Or Ray Charles or Andrea Bocelli. Or Claude Monet. Or Galileo Galilei. And countless others...

This further illustrates my hypothesis that vision is internal. The world is not external. It is our internal world that we see and experience.

What we see with our eyes is a translation of vibration. Blind people see in a different way. That is, they translate in a different way.

It is our internal world that we see and experience

Dreams and Nighttime Visions

When we are asleep at night and experience dreams, we are not seeing and experiencing with our eyes. Although we may have vivid recollections when we awaken, we did not "see" something out there in the world. We "saw" something inside of our thought world. Most of us sleep with our eyes closed, but yet dream in technicolor and through textural, emotional stories.

If the world that we see existed entirely "out there" to be "seen" with our eyes, then when we close our eyes to sleep, our world would fade to black and our dreams would not exist.

But our dreams are internal first. When we are awake, we can see and experience them "out there". Our dreams, on all levels, are internal. Your dreams for your life and for each waking day are yours and yours alone to choose.

In daily life and within a lifetime you get to deliciously experience your dreams in story form. With you as the main character, hopefully the hero or heroine, as was intended. Sometimes we see the world as our character, sometimes we see the world from a different level, one of observation.

Observation

Observation is looking at the world from a higher and wider perspective, up above and beyond this game of life that we are viscerally experiencing here. It is looking at your world through your Eyes of God.

When you see and observe at the same time, you are walking between and within the worlds. The earthly and heavenly realms. Here and now. With greater wisdom and in all of your glory, just as you intended your experience here to be.

The Different Way of Interpreting that we Call Spectrum Disorder

Just as there are different ways of "seeing" with the so-called sight-impaired or blind, some of whom have better "vision" than some sighted people, there exist other different ways of seeing too.

Stephen Wiltshire from the UK is an example of a modern genius, artist, and prodigy who is also an autistic.

"Wiltshire can look at a subject once and then draw an accurate and detailed picture of it. He frequently draws entire cities from memory, based on double, brief helicopter rides. For example, he produced a detailed drawing of four square miles of London after a single helicopter ride above that city. His nineteen-foot-long drawing of 305 square miles of New York City is based on a single twenty-minute helicopter ride."[16]

Another gentleman who "sees" and experiences life differently is Daniel Tammet. He authored the book, *Thinking in Numbers*. "In his mind, he says, each positive integer up to 10,000 has its own unique shape, colour, texture and feel."

"Tammet holds the European record for reciting pi from memory to 22,514 digits in five hours and nine minutes on 14 March 2004."

"Tammet has reportedly learned ten languages, including Romanian, Gaelic, Welsh, and Icelandic which he learned in a week for a TV documentary." [17]

There exist other geniuses and visionaries who see music or hear numbers, and experience our worlds in a different way than most of the populace perhaps.

Synesthesia occurs "when a certain sense or part of a sense is activated, another unrelated sense or part of a sense is activated concurrently. For example, when someone hears a sound, he or she immediately sees a color or shape in his or her 'mind's eye.' People that have synesthesia are called synesthetes."[18]

There are many famous synesthetes including creatives such as artists, writers, and musicians. These include Duke Ellington, Billy Joel, Itzhak Perlman, Mickey Hart, Mary J. Blige, and Pharrell Williams, to name a few brilliant musicians. Also, inventor Nikola Tesla and Physicist Richard Feynmann were said to be synesthetes.[19]

Music is a way of translating vibration. It has a sound, texture, tempo, rhythm, mood, feeling, expression and message. Just as life. Just as you do.

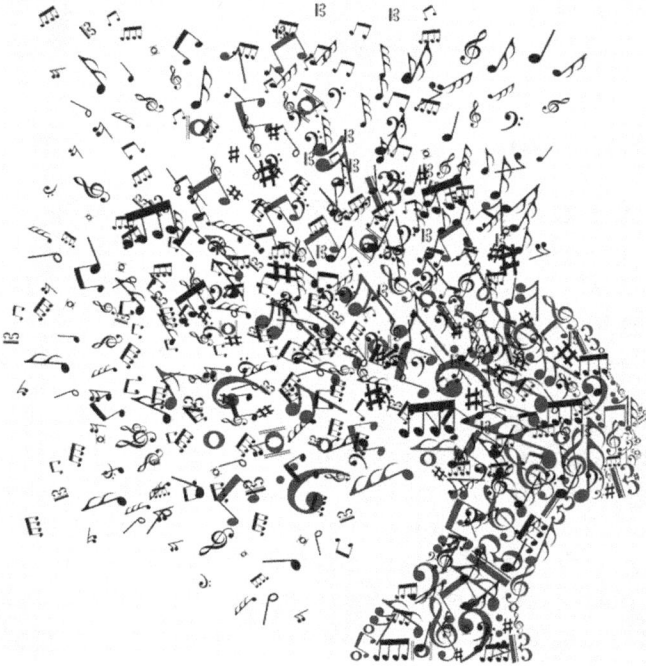

This is why artists, entertainers and musicians, those who have an innate skill with the spoken word, or with the lyrical, with the poetic, with the music, a relationship intimate with the notes, the sounds of life, are often seeing and translating from a wider spectrum, a wider point of view in general. Expressing musical language, through a vehicle such as a piano, guitar, drums, violin, or any other instrument including the instrument of voice, is genius translated into lyrical form, a universal language.

> *Music is a way of translating vibration. Music has a sound, texture, tempo, rhythm, mood, feeling, expression, and message. Just as life. Just as you do.*

Cloned Canvas

But even for all of these different ways of seeing that we have in the world, people have a tendency to flock with others who "see" in the same way. That is, people are comfortable with those who have the same viewpoints and angles on a topic. Which is natural as "like seeks like".

It is only when people see others as "wrong" because they have a differing viewpoint on an issue that they are not using their full Eyes of God. If they did, they would realize that another's differing viewpoint does not threaten them in any way. We are all here creating our own worlds. Unless you purposefully strike against another, they would not enter your experience otherwise. If you are dancing a taunting and disapproving dance with them, or a group of them, then you can expect a rumble. If you observe and know that we are all eyes of the same organism, the human condition, then your perspective widens and changes. And frees you. To be fully who *you* are.

We all assign meaning to what we see.

What we see "out there" we assign meaning to. This assigned meaning is based on what is inside of us. Our thoughts, our projections, our ideas, our imagination, our beliefs, and our learned patterns.

Just as we project our interpretations out into the world, we also function as a screen for others' interpretations. They assign meaning to us and our actions, our way, based on their beliefs and patterns. Based on what and how they see.

Results May Vary.

The caveat when we purchase a piece of equipment or assign a range of possibilities or probabilities to something, such as fuel mileage of a new vehicle, is "results may vary." And this is certainly true for everything under the sun. An identical item seen or experienced through two sets of eyes has a spectrum of meaning, value, utility, and qualities based upon our individual perceptions and expectations.

We as humans function as a living screen for other people's projections of thought and assigned meaning. This functions in the same way, whether we are watching and assigning meaning to a human's actions or story, or whether we are watching a movie screen, computer screen, or television screen. It is us looking at ourselves, assigning meaning and emotion to these stories that we *see*.

I have grouped these stratified results into seven levels that I call *The Seven Levels of Vision Development*. These are stages that we may go through to realize greater levels of self, of who we are, greater levels of expanded vision, further leading to you see more fully through your Eyes of God.

The Seven Levels of Vision Development

1. Level One: You are living in this world and think that you are your environment or a product of your environment. You react and respond to people, places, things and events in the outside world. You are completely focused on what is happening "out there" in the world, in the story of the world. Your life is based on responding and reacting to conditions that are put upon you, that you are born into, or that you find yourself in. To better your life, you look at what is going on in the outside world, or what others tell you is predicted to go on, and make rational decisions based on that. You have been taught what should make you happy by family, society or institutions. You strive to reach some of these goals in your lifetime. Your happiness is largely defined by how well you navigate the world around you. And live by other people's or society's current worldview.

2. Level Two: You may have lived on the first level for a while, perhaps a long while. You are living in this world but have a glimmer from within your soul or mind or gut reminding you that there can be more. You have goals and think through them and plan. You rely on your mind to make decisions. You weigh the pros

and cons. You look for problems to solve. You can be considered a problem solver. You now realize that there is a metaphoric box that you live in. You want to look to the edges of the box where some new ideas may live, not the center which is where the same-old, same-old, daily grind is. When you were in level one, you didn't even realize that there was a box. You just thought, "Well this is the way things are". Now you are beginning to suspect that there could be more. More to life. More for you...

3. Level Three: You realize that you have been in a dream, someone else's dream. You are learning to live by making gut decisions rather than solely decisions from your mind, your brain, your computer processing unit, your CPU. Your gut decisions, as you hone in on your attention to your own inner guidance, are proving to be right more often than your sole brain decisions. The body does not lie, your physicality has wisdom as it is the embodiment of your greater mind. You see visible positive changes in your life.

4. Level Four: Includes all of the previous journey and progressive paths. But now, you learn to live from the heart. Inspiration becomes palpable. Your life becomes more engaging and exciting for you. You add new levels of discernment - you are able to feel from your instinct, your gut. You prefer to make gut decisions. You listen to your inner guidance on topics. Even if it goes against the current or traditional wisdom. (After

all, this old wisdom was based on someone else's or familial or society's T-B-H-P.) Today is a new day.

5. Level Five: You become a changemaker in your life. Like a rebirth, you take stock of your surroundings and see if it matches your dream. The dream that you have or had long ago inside of you and forgot or stuffed down back into your soul or heart in order to be practical or to fit in or to please others or to not "rock the boat". You cannot deny your dream any longer. You must live your best life. You look at different aspects of your life, as if with new eyes. You begin to change what you see, situation by situation, for the better and for your highest joy and happiness.

6. Level Six: You become creator of your life. You refuse to live by old, outdated T-H-B-P. You have evolved to a state of power. Power always shines from within. Power is not force. Power is radiant. True power is heart-based. You expand your vision and sphere of influence. You "see" more than you ever have. And what you see is rich in texture, color, emotion, and beauty.

7. Level Seven: Creator in the world. Visionary Territory. You realize who you truly are. You see and envision as you were always meant to. As Eyes of God. You live your best and most delicious life. As was intended. As it was always meant to be for you.

You may think that we are bound by our birth and physical circumstance. Our geographical location, our race, gender, levels of abundance or family love. All of these we cannot change.

Nor would we want to. Again, it was never our intention to mourn being born into a certain point of focus. It was our intention, however, to read-write that focus and evolve it further, and to transform it and alchemize it into something new, a new experience of your creation.

> *We cause evolution to happen. As the Eyes of God,*
> *we create capers and situations where we all grow.*
> *And everyone benefits. Including who or what is*
> *behind our eyes.*

It's comedy and drama at the same time. We start life here as an infant, knowing that we are the world. We do not know that we are separate from what we see. We only see 8-10 inches at first. This is our world. We learn to see, to use our eyes and brain to translate images and our brain and heart to translate experiences. Babies and children are still so connected to who they really are, their essence; we can learn greatly. They are here to remind us of our connection to who we really are.

This is why looking into a child's or a baby's eyes is so precious. It is looking at purity.

Then, we grow and develop and differentiate ourselves from the world. This happens so we can experience our worlds, see and feel what it is all about.

We experience our projections, see and feel what they are, how they can be improved. We listen to our inner GPS, our guidance, and follow that path. The path that we have set out for ourselves. We evolve our family patterns, meaning we evolve our way of being, the output of our software projections. From 1.0 to 2.0 to infinite improved versions. We've come a long way and are on a never-ending evolutionary path as human beings.

We are living holograms of our thoughts.

We realize that we are the projectors. That the world is a projection of us! If we don't like what we see, then we can load a new movie onto the projector. Think old-time reel film projectors, or DVDs or streaming video. Or a click on your computer, device, iPad, Kindle or smartphone to a new story, a new visual, a new experience.

We create life in a new and improved way, one of our choosing. Our world is the world. We are seven billion individual creators living in seven billion unique worlds of our creation. Experiencing them and enjoying them to the degree that we realize that we are the man/woman/person behind the curtain, the ghost in the machine, the pantheon of gods in the sky, the greater eye behind the I, the greater I behind the eye.

We have come full circle to realize the orientation of who we are. Like the newborn who is still so connected to source she doesn't know yet that she is separate, we too remember this knowledge. But as we go we have taken our version of life and have been given the opportunity to improve upon it. To create a more beautiful version of what we first were born into. To love it into being.

It is all about vision and how you see life. You project your thoughts into a vision, your version of life, your world. This is what you see. Because you are the projector behind the eyes. You are seeing your own movie.

> *It is all about vision and how you see life. You project your thoughts into a vision, your version of life, your world. This is what you see. Because you are the projector behind the eyes. You are seeing your own movie.*

You are not seeing what is "out there", you are seeing what is in here, inside of you, your thought world, your beliefs, patterns, interpretations, expectations, desires and fears. You are seeing, in a visual format and context, the frequency of your thoughts. You are experiencing your thoughtmind in a different way of translation. You are looking at it visually. You are looking in a mirror.

Your life and what you make of it - is all about your specific and individual vision. How clearly you can see yourself translates into how clearly you can see, thus experience, the world. If you are full of shadows, then this is what you will see out there. The shadows are not you, of course, they were recorded there earlier on, by a world that was accustomed to seeing shadows. The only way to see with more clarity is to shine the light on the clouded or shadowy areas.

Then you will see who you really are. In all of your glory. For you are the Eyes of God.

Chapter Two: Improve Your Vision:
Vision Questions and Exercises

- Do you have 20/20 vision with your physical eyes? If not, do you see any correlation with your outer vision and inner thoughts, habits or patterns?

- Do you love what you see? What don't you love? If not, why? What is the gift in it for you?

- Where are you farsighted in life? Are you missing out on important and joyous things that are very close to you? Is there something that you don't want to see? Where can you shine the light out there that would shed light for you on a topic that is currently uncomfortable to see? *Hint: Shining the light will ultimately make it less dark and shadowy, more manageable, easier to look at, discern, and maybe even learn from, and to see and receive the gift in it for you.*

- Where are you nearsighted in life? Are you caring for yourself, your needs, your passions, your heart, body, mind and soul in the way that you truly desire? And deserve to? Where can you shine the light on yourself, on which parts of your life, to see yourself more in all of your true glory, the unique beautiful individual who you indeed are? *Do that!*

  It was never our intention to mourn being born into a certain point of focus. It <u>was</u> our intention to *read-write that focus and evolve it further, and to transform it, to alchemize it into something new, a new experience of your own creation.*

How your life began is the metaphorical clay that you have been given to work with. The beauty of the sculpture is up to you as artist.

CHAPTER 3
You as Creator Being

Spectators, Participators, and Creators

There are three types of people and three levels of experience and engagement here in this world: Spectators, Participators, and Creators. We each are a combination of all of these, with usually one being dominant. The orientation may differ, in a larger sense, from how we live daily within our vantage points. These can change throughout our lives as we define how we want to live at any point in time.

These differing levels of orientation and of engagement provide different experiences for you.

Spectators

A spectator is predominantly an observer in the world. A spectator is happy to sit on the sidelines and watch life. We are all spectators in some ways. When we watch sports, appreciate art, or view others' creations, these are all fine ways to provide enjoyment for ourselves. And to learn, grow, appreciate, laugh, cry, cheer, enjoy, and smile. It is a more passive way of providing happiness for ourselves. However, if we are *only* spectators then life may be not as fulfilling as it could be if we actively engage on some levels.

Linda LaFlamme

Being in the role of an observer, a spectator, provides enjoyment to our lives and appreciation for others' efforts and creations. This is an important way of being in many situations. But optimally, not in all situations.

A spectator watches and views others' creations in the world. He looks at those as the world.

Spectator Attributes

- *Characteristics* - A spectator role is the most passive of the three types. He observes life in this world. He may like or dislike what he sees and he acknowledges the world as a static place with rules and limitations. He dislikes a higher percentage of what he sees compared to the other two types. He is the least discerning of the three about what he includes in his world via experiences, media, thoughts, people and situations.

- *Motivations* - He is motivated by comfort, security and familiarity. And who doesn't love these. He is not motivated by change, progress or effort though. He carries the most fear of the three. Because he feels powerless to make any changes in the world. He has not discovered his true power. Yet.

- *Point of View* - A spectator lives in what he calls reality. He feels that he is born into a world and then he looks for the best ways to adapt to that world. The world may be a cruel place or it may be a happy place. But in any case, it is the world he was born into and it is what it is. You can't change the world, right?

- *Possible History* - During the Recorder Stage he was taught that life is as it is. You are born here and then you make your way. He felt limitation put upon him or his family or any group that he identified with, either directly or via osmosis. If he is a dominant spectator in his life, he may have been taught, incorrectly, that he is nothing special. He was taught that the way to happiness is to fit in, to not misbehave, to not upset the status quo - of the family or out there in the world.

- *World Sphere* - He observes and then fits into the box of life that he sees. He feels the most limited of the three. He has no idea that there even is a box to his world or a limit to his way of thought. If one is primarily a spectator then he still is somewhat of a Recorder; he is subject to others impressing their dysfunction and peculiarities and viewpoints onto him.

- *Sphere of Influence* - He has a limited sphere of influence as he is observing most of the time. He may complain or compliment, likely more often complain, but he is happy to have friends to commiserate with and who understand him (other spectators with the same worldview). He feels that others are born with advantages that he wasn't, that life is not fair, that life, money, and abundance, are limited and must be divided up. Some people unfairly get more. Others suffer without, because life is the way it is, you can't change it, it is reality.

- *Next Steps* - If one is dominantly a spectator, he could open his mind to the possible thought that there is more out there. That maybe he has more power inside, untapped, than he realized. That, maybe just maybe, he is more than he has been taught...

- *Positive Areas/Utilization* - There is a time and place for putting on our spectator goggles for optimal vision and experience. The spectator way of being is great when we want to appreciate this world and others' creations within it. Examples include appreciating art or media, observing nature, listening to music, watching artistic creations on the movie screen, large and small. Or walking through daily life. We would not want to be without this way of seeing because we would not have the chance to savor or view, to take a step back, to take an in-breath of all of the beauty that we see. A spectator can use his Eyes of God to shine a loving light on beauty and creations in this world. This can be incredibly powerful.

- *Application* - If we are primarily or dominantly spectators, though, we could be depriving ourselves of actually experiencing life to the fullest. It is one thing to research on the internet or to read a book about playing a sport or walking on the beach. But it is another thing to actually experience it. To experience the feelings, the joys that this world has to offer - to participate.

- *Vision Index* - 3 out of 10. A spectator sees the world and experiences life. Although it is the life that others have created, the world that he has been taught to see.

Participators

A participator takes an active role in experiences that he desires to engage in. Playing sports is an example. A participator adds his own brand of magic to enhance a creation in progress. This may be furthering the work of his company, his community, or for a larger goal or purpose that he is aligned with. (A *participator* is a general way of being. A *participant* takes part in a specific activity.)

A participator is engaged in life. He does not sit on the sidelines generally. He is more content to be in the game rather than watching the game.

We learn by experience. It is one thing for someone to tell you what love is, but to experience it yourself is quite another matter. All the words or sights or sounds cannot match the delicious, soul-stirring experience of being *in* it. Love.

It is important to choose and to be selective about what you participate in. Many of us think we are obligated to certain situations in life. If these situations do not bring us joy or make our heart sing, then perhaps it is time to re-evaluate how we participate in those activities. It's always a good practice to take stock now and then to see how your life could be improved, how it can bring you greater joy. Maybe more free time would bring you greater joy, maybe greater abundance, or spending your time differently. It is up to you to decide what works best for you and then make that happen. Get in the game. Participate!

Participator Attributes

- *Characteristics* - A participator role is more active than that of the spectator. He wants to get into the game and play. He knows that he can enjoy experiences here in this world, can advance in his career, and can make a difference. He is more selective about what he includes in his world via experiences, media, thoughts, people and situations.

- *Motivations* - He is motivated by experiences, the feeling that certain experiences provide, progress, winning and he may be somewhat competitive. He carries less fear than the spectator does, and he can view his desires to be greater than his fear, thus allowing himself to reach new levels.

- *Point of View* - A participator looks for ways to improve his world. He knows that he has latitude in improving his lot in life and making his experiences better. He wants to win at the game called life and enjoy what he desires most at any point in time.

- *Possible History* - During the Recorder Stage he may have been taught that he was important and valued. He knew through osmosis that he could make a difference in his life. He may have had teachers or mentors in his early life who taught him that he could go far in the world. The world is what it is and you can make it better.

- *World Sphere* - The participator knows that he can jump into a game, the game of life, the games of the world, and make a contribution.

- *Sphere of Influence* - He has a greatly expanded sphere of influence in comparison with the spectator. He may complain or compliment, and seeks mentors or others' points of view to further his causes. He has buttons to push and reacts in situations when people "push his buttons". He receives lucky breaks, knows that he must prepare for opportunity when it knocks, and appreciates progressive thinking. He likely believes on some level that jobs, clients, and abundance are in a static amount and must be divided up and he wants to get his share of the pie. And he hopes or knows that if he works hard, he can do it. You can make a better lot in life for yourself and for your children through smart decisions, hard work and effort.

- *Next Steps* - If one is dominantly a participator, he could further progress to the evolutionary point of realizing that, rather than striving to win in the game, someone else's game, he could create his own game.

- *Positive Areas/Utilization* - The participator experience is where we live much of our lives. We actually get to enjoy, savor, stretch ourselves and our abilities, learn, and dig into life. We participate in, do the things that we enjoy. Rather than merely watching the game all of the time, we are playing in the game too and this can be very satisfying. We are using our senses here to jump into life and we love being here. Participating can be a very satisfying and savory experience.

- *Application* - If we are primarily or dominantly participators, we are striving to enjoy life and to improve our life and the lives of our families. But there is an even greater level to expand within, a realm to jump into. And that is the realm of creator.

- *Vision Index* - 6 out of 10. A participator is not afraid to jump into the game of life. He works within the framework here that was set forth and strives to make improvements and grab his piece of the pie. He sees much farther than the spectator and likes to think outside the box, the current framework he lives within.

Note: Pronouns She and He are used interchangeably here and throughout entire book. Gender of any form does not play a role in any of our examples as seen through the Eyes of God,

Creators

A creator has the potential to attain the highest level of vision and knowing at a point in time. A creator knows that the world is his oyster and creates his life from his vision of how he wants it to be.

As an example, on an intimate level, lovemaking from a spectator's point of view, not quite like the real thing. Being a participator is much more delicious. However, actively creating a romantic evening, or lifetime, for you and your beloved may bring a whole new level of soul satisfaction.

Applied in a work setting, one clocking in reluctantly to a regular job they very much dislike may be on the spectator's workday calendar. Working toward that promotion or even corner office with great perks may be on the participator's agenda. While, jumping over to a new level, creating that opportunity, starting that business, inventing that item, expressing themselves artistically or creatively, living their life the way they want on their terms, may be on the creator's mind.

Creator Attributes

- *Characteristics* - A creator is the most active way of being. He knows that he can create his life the way he wants it and he will see it reflected back to him. When he believes it, he will see it. It may take more or less time, but see it he will. He creates his circumstance, knows himself deeply, and makes the most positive contribution he can in the world. He knows that the world he sees is of his own making. He is not merely reacting to the world, he is making it happen, he is creating it as he goes along. If he doesn't like what he sees, he knows it is in his power to improve his vision and thus his experience of life.

- *Motivations* - He is motivated by creating the best life possible. This life is defined by him. He is not at whim of others' desires for him to fit in to what they want for him or how they think he should be, nor is he interested in what boxes the world may want to put him into. He wants to and will create his best life. This creation includes for himself and for his family, it could be for his community or the world. Positive experiences, new expressions, new horizons, evolutionary thought, personally and for humanity, motivate the creator.

- *Point of View* - A creator knows that he makes his own opportunities, his own path, and his own experience. There is no winning or losing, as this is an abundant world. Each of us live in our own versions of the world. His worldview is one of abundance, not scarcity. There is no pie to split up. He is interested in creating more pie. There is unlimited pie. As creators, we create the pie. Oftentimes for ourselves and others too. Therefore, he is not interested in taking someone else's pie. That is so… yesterday, not evolutionary.

- *Possible History* - During the Recorder Stage he likely had one of two experiences. Either he was born into a family of projectors who were of creator orientation, thus impressing this worldview onto him. Or, he was born into a situation so adverse that he had two choices - delve into hell. Or create heaven. And he chose to create heaven. Often it is the latter of these two experiences that mould the creator.

"Of the billionaires on the 2013 Forbes 400 list, 273 qualify as "self-made." The fact that nearly three-quarters of the ultra-wealthy individuals highlighted on this year's list began their lives in circumstances far different than the ones they now occupy might be seen a testament to the kind of access and mobility that is the basis of the American dream."[20]

There is a surprising and inordinate percentage of billionaires who rose from adverse circumstance.

I simply love the quote from Larry Ellison, successful billionaire, philanthropist, adventurer and creator of his own destiny. The quote is, "I have had all of the disadvantages required for success." And his early life shaped his fortitude and desire to succeed and create on a global scale. As did Steve Jobs. As did Oprah's. As have countless others who have made and continue to make a positive global impact from within their lives.

Even the parable stories of Jesus, Moses, Buddha and other religious figures also carry these same notes of hardship, love (for self and others), and shining their brilliance so that others could realize theirs.

This is what a creator _does_. This is why they are singled out in their respective religions as seeing on a wide scale with their full Eyes of God. This is why they are a revered example to so many people the world over.

Additional attributes of a Creator:

- *World Sphere* - The creator creates his world.

- *Sphere of Influence* - Unlimited. There are no limits to a creator's sphere of influence. If you dream it, you can do it.

- *Next Steps* - You decide. It is all up to you! What do you want to create?

- *Positive Areas/Utilization* - Changing the world, making the world the best expression of progress and love that you can. Seeing the world as a whole of creation. Seeing far and wide. Seeing pleasing creations. Experiencing beauty. Seeing love.

- *Vision Index* - 8-10 out of 10. A creator knows who he is and sees the world in the highest and best expression.

There are no organic differences between the spectator, participator, and creator. Only their vantage point. If a spectator wants to be more engaged in certain areas, it is only a matter of shifting his perspective, turning toward the direction of what he wants, and jumping into life with both feet to be more of a participator. Or maybe starting by dipping his toe in and then his foot. Sometimes this can be scary or bring up fears, rational and irrational, real or imagined, usually imagined. But you will never know, unless you dip your toe in, how great the water can be.

There is no difference between a creator, a visionary, and anyone else on this blue planet.

Why? Because - you *are* a creator. It is your innate nature, your essence. You just maybe hadn't realized it yet in the fullest sense ... We are all creators. The degree to which you exercise this is up to you.

What would you like to create?

> *We were all born with the Eyes of God. Only some of us don't know it yet. They have not seen themselves as who they truly are. And are truly meant to be.*

We Awaken...

~

New Day

Upon awakening in the morning our consciousness emerges back into our bodies - we become slowly or quickly aware that we are here in this world, our world. We slowly or quickly come back into awareness, depending on the manner in which we are awakened, ranging from something jarring or discordant, maybe an alarm clock, or gently on our own. We pass through the dream world quickly, the world of quantum mental thoughtform soup, passing through and remembering our dreams as we enter into more awareness. We interpret this world of thoughtform into a scenario that is relevant to us. These interpretations trigger feelings in us, emotions, relating to the energy that is swirling around us. The energy that we have created and are emanating and experiencing. We stretch, open our eyes, and greet the day. The day filled with our consciousness, our perspective. It is a new day.

~

Enlightening Our Lives/Enlightenment/Quantum Leaps

Upon awakening in life our consciousness becomes vivid within our bodies - we become slowly or quickly aware that we are here in this world, our world. We slowly or quickly come back into awareness, depending on the manner in which we are awakened, ranging from something discordant or jarring, health crises, personal hurdles, addictions, our darkest hours and dark nights, or gently on our own. Through meditation, yoga, love, inspiration, or following our dreams, connecting to our essence within, seeing ourselves. We pass through the dream world quickly, passing through and remembering our dreams as we enter into more awareness. We interpret this world of thoughtform into a scenario that is relevant to us. These interpretations trigger feelings in us, emotions, relating to the energy that is swirling around us. The energy that we have created and are emanating and experiencing. We stretch, open our eyes, and greet the day. The day filled with our consciousness, our perspective. It is a new day. We have new knowledge.

~

Birth

For birth and in our growing years our consciousness emerges into our bodies - we become slowly or quickly aware that we are here in this world, our world. We slowly or quickly come into awareness, depending on the manner in which we are awakened, ranging from a slap on the bottom, a water birth, or other welcoming to this world. We pass through the dream world quickly, passing through and remembering our dreams as we enter into more awareness. We interpret this world of thoughtform into a scenario that is relevant to us. These interpretations trigger feelings in us, emotions, relating to the energy that is swirling around us. The energy that has been created around us in our environment. First we learn, mimic and observe. We learn about life here and about love through our parents or caregivers. This is learned on the energetic vibrational level. Actions not words. Thoughts and intentions above actions. As we grow and as time goes on here, we create, emanate, and experience. We stretch, open our eyes and greet the day. The day filled with our consciousness, our perspective. It is a new day. It is a new life.

~

Transition of Form/Death

Upon awakening on another level of our consciousness, our focus emerges back into our larger awareness - who we really are - we become slowly or quickly aware that we are here in this world, our world, the greater world, the all that is. We slowly or quickly come back into awareness, depending on the manner in which we are awakened, ranging from something jarring or discordant, such as an "accident", or gently on our own. We pass through the dream world quickly, the world of quantum mental thoughtform soup, passing through, up, and remembering our dreams as we enter into more awareness. We interpret this world of thoughtform into a scenario that is relevant to us. These interpretations trigger feelings in us, emotions, relating to the energy that is swirling around us. The energy that we have created and are emanating and experiencing. We may see a bright light or our loving relatives. We continue. Only now, we see from a much wider vantage point, a vast universe, from the totality of our being. We stretch, open our mind's eye fully, and greet the day. We remember who we really are. The day filled with our full consciousness, our perspective. Which is love. It is a new day. A perpetual day, with no night to contrast the full light. And it is good.

And so... it continues. The cycle begins anew. The wheel turns. But with new joys, new possibilities.

New joys, new possibilities... for _you_.

Enjoy your time here on terra firma. Expand your vision to create your highest and best expression in your life right here and now in the present. What joys do you want to experience?

Vision and Perspective

Our dreams are personal. We cannot dream for anyone else. And what we dream including our desires are our own.

In the dreamworld at night or in our visions during the day, these visual escapades, movies, translations of thoughtform, are personal to us. They are personal to our own perceptions, desires, understandings of how the (our) world works, and to the thoughtforms, waves, we have going on that comprise our mental activity. This is based on our world as we know it to be. Our world as we are creating it.

Our dreams for our lives are personal to us also. No one can dream for us. Although others can communicate, directly and indirectly, what they want for us, how they want us to behave, what they want or expect from us, they cannot emanate for us and live our lives. We are the only ones who decide how our lives will go, down which paths, and with which companions. We may think that we ought to do something or follow someone else's desires for us, but in reality we are the ones making those decisions, one by one. Someone can lead you by the hand, or drag you by the collar, but it is you and you alone who has the final say about your actions, inactions, desires for yourself, and walking the path that you choose. Live *your* dreams for your life. This is sacred living and you always know the way. It is known by how you feel inside about which path you are on, which avenues to take, and the joy that it brings to you.

This is how all successful visionary leaders, personally in their lives and on a wider scale, make the large differences in the world that they do. They envision with clarity, are driven by their passions about a particular path, and pioneer ahead. Oftentimes they forge ahead solely, as theirs is a road less traveled. Or not traveled yet. It is for them to explore and pave the way. For their own happiness and as a brightly shining torch for others. By pioneering a new way, creating an idea, offering something of benefit, others benefit too.

When an idea benefits us, we want to embrace it. A visionary creates, materializes, manifests, and concretizes their vision. And the more beautiful, progressive, and beneficial it is, other thought leaders then embrace it. This is how societal evolution occurs.

This goes back to my statement earlier. If something brings you joy, it is leading you to your right path. If a visionary has a burning passion to give life to an idea, to create a business, a company, a product, a new way about something, it is usually because they see the benefit of the idea. It is not the idea itself for the idea's sake - it is for the benefits behind the idea. The benefits may include making life easier for individuals or society, maybe it will provide abundance or joy for people, bring happiness, save people time thus allowing more life enjoyment, or solve existing issues for individuals or on a societal scale. No matter which industry one is in, be it selling products of any sort, personal services or B2B services, entertainment, technology, or other, the same principle applies. New ideas, products, services, companies, and evolution, all take place because a visionary had an idea that they knew and felt would be beneficial to those using the product, service or idea, or to the world at large.

Ideas spread because people benefit and then become enthusiastic and passionate about them too. In the introductory phase for especially disruptive, evolutionary ideas, first there is a backlash, resistance by the old guard. The old guard of old thoughtforms of habits (T-H-B-P). And then the ideas are embraced and accepted and applauded. Is your idea disruptive enough to be evolutionary?

Variety

We are all individual projectors, projecting our own wants, desires, hang-ups, peculiarities, passions, dreams and fears. We are projecting and seeing different angles and with different lenses. We didn't come here to be all the same. We came to explore and to enjoy.

Without the variety in our world and that we are born into, and the seeming polar opposites, we would not have a baseline to create new desires and dreams.

This is why you were born. To immerse, to jump into the pool of differentiation and variation, joy and fear, love and the absence of, ease and difficulty.... To make a difference. To make *your* positive difference here.

What if everything was already done? How would we know what feels good, if the opposite does not exist. You are here to be a beacon of shining light to your world, your life. When you do this and live in this way, continually evolving and shining more light, shining your brilliance, on everyone and with everything that you do... when you do this... your (the) world changes.

Be the creator that you were meant to be, that you <u>are</u>. Start now.

> *Everything you can imagine is real.*
> *Picasso*

The only way that we can ever change our world...is not by changing others; It is only by changing ourselves and what we emanate. Thus what we see.

We don't have to wait for the world to change to live our best life. We create our own world.

Don't "see" things into being that you don't want.

If you are focusing on something, you are raising the possibility or probability that it may materialize in your life. Choose wisely. Focus on what you want. Focus on what feels best to you. If you see something in your mind's eye, worry about an outcome, and do not like what you see... change your thought and focus on a better outcome, one that you would like to see. You will raise the probability that you will see that instead. What do you want? Look at that. Look in that direction.

Chapter Three: Expand Your Vision: Vision Questions and Exercises

- What do you want within and for your life's journey? What are your unique talents and passions? Why not go out for a quiet walk or spend some time in nature and ask yourself the following: Why are you here? Why are <u>you</u> here? Why are you <u>here</u>? When you were a child what did you find fun? What are you passionate about? What brings you the most joy? What are the greatest desires for your life?

- From your answers above, make your positive desires a focused thought/pattern. Envision it. See it into being.

- You now know how the world that you see comes into being. By changing the way you view the world, the world appears different. It reveals itself to you in a different way. Be the visionary creator you were born to be.

- T-H-B-P Exercise (Thought-Habit-Belief-Pattern)

  T - *Thought* - Your ideas of a better life. What would you like to see? What would you like your life story to be?

  H - *Habit* - Every morning when you wake up take 10 minutes to envision and feel your world as you would like it to unfold. Do this before going to sleep too. Let this feeling become a habit.

B - *Belief* - Choose a new viewpoint, a higher altitude to view old, discordant situations from. Know who you *really* are. A creator.

P - *Pattern* - Live authentically and shine your brilliance.

CHAPTER 4
The Meaning of Life and Your Story

We give life meaning

Life is a series of images and projections. Our interpretations create meaning. And this is how we experience our world. On their own these images do not have a particular meaning, but we are the ones who give life meaning. It is "what" we see and "how" we see, and "how much we see" that gives our subjects meaning.

We may see a stone on our path or a bird calling to us and assign it meaning... the scent of a rose reminds us of romance. The smells of certain foods remind you of your childhood. These experiences make our lives rich, they provides texture and backdrop for our delicious story.

Also the alphabet, with any alphabet... the letters or characters are just particular squiggles on a page. But we assign to them, the squiggles, meaning. Based on collective agreement. And we group them together to form words to assign even greater complexities of meaning. And certain groups of people on the planet speak and read different languages. So they understand each other better than those who view different squiggles of meaning.

> *B: Wow you look phat.*
> *G: What? How dare you?*
> *B: I was giving you a compliment.*

G: *If you think I'm fat then at least don't say it.*
Sheesh
(* Merriam -Webster Dictionary, phat: very attractive or appealing)

-

I remember in French class in junior high school I
wrote a skit that went something like this... Two
Americans go into a restaurant in Paris and sit down
to order. Wanting to order the daily catch fish
special, the person showing off their French
language skills (learned in the week before the trip)
says, "I'll order the poisson", (pr. pwa-sson) which
is French for fish. Mistakenly pronouncing it as pwa-
zon poison. A lethal mistake. Especially to the
annoyed French waiter, who the diner had already
called over as garçon while snapping his fingers.
Well, you may guess the end, as the waiter dutifully
brought out a bottle with a skull and crossbones on it,
signifying universally that it was not the daily catch.

We assign meaning to language, words, lines and
squiggles. And to all that we see. Sometimes others
understand those exact squiggles and words in the same
way. Other times not.

We have a collective understanding of ideas, themes,
archetypes, and memes. These are based on the human
condition that we all share. Some symbols have regional or
universal meaning.

It is not that life is meaningless. Hardly. Quite the opposite.
It is full of depth and meaning. It is just that the meaning is

individual and subjective. Based on the information that we have extrapolated for our own individual worlds. Our lives are what we want to make of them.

We get to decide about and enjoy all of the delicious textures and flavors of our life experiences. This is why we are here.

The meaning of life is individual and subjective.

> *You are on a delicious and exciting journey of your own story, with your own desires, your own quest, your own hero's journey. And, in the process, you may quite possibly change the world indelibly for the better.*

Objective and Subjective

We only use a fraction of our brains it has been reported in certain studies. However as you know studies can say anything and can make anything appear to be true or not true, based on factors including the agenda of the study, what the eyes behind the study want to "see" and the observer effect. I feel that the observer effect is not merely some random factor, but a factor that is essential to our new understanding of vision. In fact, the observer effect exists with everything. Because everything is subjective, there are really no objective thoughts or beliefs. I would posit that our experience of life, and of everything that we see, is subjective.

Remember, when we got here to this planet we were like Recorders, human hard drives and had to learn to use our eyes, as discussed earlier in the human development chapter. And we mimicked patterns, thoughts, family, peers, and society around us.

Now objectivists would argue with me about subjectivity here. However, let me say that an objectivist belief, in and of itself, is subjective. Not everybody shares an objectivist belief. An objectivist belief, or any belief, was built upon extrapolating data and coming to one's own conclusions based on the lens that they are looking through, in, or out. And the amount of light (or spectrum of information) that they are allowing through. What they are allowing through is then translated into a projection or vibratory movie - out there.

Proof and Reality

We can prove anything to ourselves that we want, because we project it mentally. And then we think it is a result of something out there. When in reality it is a result of something inside. Some aspect of us, one way of looking at things, that is quite literally "one way of looking at things". One angle, one point of view. We see what we are. Really, and quite literally.

> *We "see", that is we project, something and then assign meaning to it. As you now know, this is how our eye/brain systems work. With the help and*

*compass of our GPS (our inner guidance, what I
call our God Positioning System). And our inner
unique purpose, our raison d'être, that moves us
along.*

And if we don't like something that we see in our world,
then it is a cue that we have some outdated belief that
probably wasn't ours to begin with, that we can change.

What is often the case though, with people who don't have
this knowledge, which has been a majority of people on the
planet... people don't like what they see and then they
begin tilting at windmills. They throw barbs at some aspect
of themselves that they don't want to see or acknowledge.
They throw darts at their own reflections of something
inside of them. They shoot bullets at some aspect of
themselves.

Everything must begin at home. Everything must start with
you. There is no other way. There is no way to change the
world unless you change your projection of the world.

The world is our creation. As an adult, the world that you
see can be of your creation.

*Use your Eyes of God to create the world that you want to
see. The power lies in the love behind your eyes.*

Deja Vu

Have you ever experienced "déjà vu"? You are in the middle of a situation and, suddenly, you get the distinct feeling that you have been there before, in exactly that same place, with the same people, in the midst of the same conversation. What is this phenomenon?

Did you dream the situation? Were you actually there before? Was this destiny?

Yes. No. And maybe.

You feel that you have been there before because you have - somewhere in your imagination, in your thought world. This may have been on a subconscious level so it is not concretely recognizable as something that has happened in physical life prior. Just in the thought world. Which is where everything is created before we see it here in visible physical form.

When you experience déjà vu you are experiencing a knowing, a knowing of something that was and is now on your path, a probable occurrence, based on your creations within your subconscious, your world of thought.

How delicious it is to dream of your lover or spouse, or perfect vacation, a delicious meal, a new business, your ideal home, your joyful work in the world... and then "see" it come to fruition. Discover it, experience it, feel the emotion contained within the seed essence of it.

Blind Spots

In our daily lives, we have all had the experience of looking for a "lost" object. We look, turn over papers, look in drawers, retrace our steps, and then, lo and behold, there it is, we "find" it. And we smile as it was in front of us all along, we just didn't see it. These are our blind spots.

Just as when we don't see something in our lives that all of our friends and those closest to us see. They mention it, we still do not and cannot see it. ... *Until we do.*

By seeing more clearly and fully, you will begin to see through and beyond those blind spots. Shining light onto them, bringing a smile to your face.

Visibility and Invisibility

With our physical eye vision we know that we have a blind spot for each eye.

"... the blind spot, physiological blind spot, 'blind point', or punctum caecum in medical literature, is the place in the visual field that corresponds to the lack of light-detecting photoreceptor cells on the optic disc of the retina where the optic nerve passes through the optic disc. Since there are no cells to detect light on the optic disc, a part of the field of vision is not perceived. The brain interpolates the blind spot based on surrounding detail and information from the other eye, so the blind spot is not normally perceived".[21]

If you read the above again you will understand that the brain provides you with data based on information it is translating from the other eye and surroundings. In other words, it is making up a story to fill in the gap of your blind spot, based on the information it is decoding and processing. And this may be based on expected experience or past experience, logical experience to you.

We as humans also have blind spots when it comes to life and our interpretation of it. It seems that when we are expecting something, we see it more easily. In other instances we may see something that isn't really there as our minds are trained by habit, pattern or belief to see such a thing, to fill in that gap, for our blind spot.

Here's a quick exercise to try. The next time that you "lose" something, try this. The item has not disappeared from the world. Although it has disappeared from *your* world, from your field of vision... but only for the moment. The more you think it is "lost" the less likely you will be able to easily "find" it, meaning "see" it. If you tell yourself and know and feel that you will find it, then it will be much easier and quicker to "find".

Blind Spots, Translating Light and Seeing Shadows

Parallel and symbolically, in your eyes where you have photoreceptor cells in your employ, the broader range and periphery spectrum that you can figuratively see, and the more expansive your vision, the less chance for blind spots, which are filled in by T-H-B-P. This is dependent upon the amount of light that you can translate. Or, as I hypothesize as a parallel, can project through you from your Eyes of God. Where you are lacking metaphoric photoreceptor cells, converting light into signals, you have a blind spot. You are seeing a shadow and assigning meaning, as your mind is filling in from T-H-B-P, what seems logical to you with the patterns that you have.

"A photoreceptor cell is a specialized type of neuron found in the retina (i.e., rods and cones) that is capable of phototransduction. The great biological importance of photoreceptors is that they convert light (visible electromagnetic radiation) into signals that can stimulate biological processes."[22]

> *Regarding blind spots, the brain provides you with data based on information it is translating from the other eye and surroundings. In other words, it is making up a story to fill in the gap of your blind spot, based on the information it is decoding and processing. And this may be based on expected experience or past experience, logical experience to you.*

Near Death Visions and Experiences

There exist many documented near-death experiences. Some people see religious figures particular to their own religion. In other words, Christians may see Jesus and receive messages. They may see angels. Atheists may see a bright light.[23]

In research I came across an article that discussed people's accounts of experiencing heaven and hell during near death experiences. The article asked, *"Is Hell Real?"*[24] I would say, "Yes, for those people who experienced it." But I would also remind that our experiences are subjective. They are based on a person's thought world and programs that they have playing in the background of their thought-minds. It is an interpretation, their interpretation, of their own inner world of beliefs, fears, and thought patterns. It is not relevant to anyone else as everyone has their own beliefs and thought patterns which vary and differ.

In some altered state experiences (visionquest, fasting, meditation, substance induced or enhanced), people may see their own deceased relatives. Some people see a white light. Some people see patterns of light. Some people see spirits and ghosts. Some people see space aliens. But not all. If one does not believe in ghosts or space aliens, it would be a stretch to see these, as their brain does not have a reference point or a belief system to support a vision as such. Are these real? Yes, to those people who are seeing them.

What is real?

What we see is an interpretation of vibration from our thought world. If we do not have those thoughts that others do then it is unlikely that we will see visions that are not in line with our thought parameters, our paradigms, and our belief systems. Which we have the ability to choose or change.

> *The joy and breadth of our lives and our experiences of them, our individual stories, are based on our vision spectrum that we allow ourselves to have and cultivate.*

> *You project your world through your Eyes of God.*

Focus

Sometimes people can get so lost and disconnected from who they really are that they are off-course completely. They are heading in the opposite direction of their destiny, their dreams. You can see this all around, just watch the news for a few minutes.

But it never has to be this way.

These temporarily lost people were perhaps trained when they were young by parents who were trained when they were young, by parents who were trained when they were young, to look to someone else to tell them the way their life should go. This is appropriate when we are children, but when we are adults we can choose our own destinies. This 'old way of looking at things' habit takes your focus off of the road in front of you - and puts your focus elsewhere. This will not get you to where your soul wants you to go, or at least it will be a veering off-course or a longer route that it needs to be. But, if it is not your true direction but the direction of others, even well-meaning others, you can change direction at any time. All it takes is changing your focus.

This is true for anything. If you don't like what you see, change your focus to something else, look in a different direction, one that *you* want to go in and toward.

The secret to getting and staying on the right path is to look forward without too much distraction of others' T-H-B-P. It's easier than you think. All you need to do is point yourself in the right direction. And your focus will bring life to your road. You do not need to struggle on down the road. You do not need to run down the road either, for you will be given a vehicle to take yourself down that road. These vehicles may take the form of a job, an experience, hobbies, serendipitously meeting new like-minded visionaries such as yourself, as just a few examples of infinite possibilities. You will attract to you the methods and the madness to get you to where you want to go.

When I first took natural horsemanship lessons, I was told to look in the direction where you want to go and the horse will naturally go in that direction. Why is this? Because you are focused on what you want and the horse is a natural to understanding energy flow so he will understand your desire or silent command. This works in the same way with anything that you are steering, driving, riding or even on your own power. The brilliance of inventor and entrepreneur Dean Kamen, shines always and shone when he channeled this focus into the design of the Segway PT, which is "commanded" to move based on where your body focus is. Tilt or lean in one direction, the PT will go that way. If you are driving a car, you need to look where you are going. If you are distractedly looking all around (*Look, a shiny thing...or... Oh, I just got a text.*) then "accidents" have more of a likelihood of happening. These accidents are an indication that you veered from your path. Often what we call an unfortunate "accident" is something that occurred while you were looking someplace else, while you were focused on something else, while doing some other thing. You took your focus away from what was important. It really is all about vision.

Sometimes accidents occur when we go against our own gut feeling, our inner guidance. So we are looking in a direction opposite to where our inner guidance is telling us to look.

For when we follow our inner guidance and wisdom and know the direction where we want to go, then we are guided to the most expeditious way to get there. You know how if you look even slightly to the right while driving you have the natural tendency to veer in that direction, to the right. Subtle, but this knowledge makes all the difference in the world. When you look in distraction away from your intended direction and path, thus causing you to veer slightly, your whole course of direction can be changed.

Of course someone may honk their horn at you in the right lane next to you. "Thank you for the wake-up call. I was veering", you may say to yourself. This is a gift. A reminder. Listen to the subtle cues. Easier than veering off the road into a ditch or worse, changing your whole life course in the direction that you didn't intend to go in.

You can change course now or at any point in time to go in your intended direction.

And when you're driving you don't look back constantly either. You are focused on where you are going. Otherwise it could be a slow, rough or even painful journey. But it never needs to be.

And, your focus of vision is matched to your sphere of influence at any given time. If you are talking personally with a friend or loved one your focus is mainly right in front of you, intense and personal. If you are talking with a large group, your focus is wider, encompassing more in your field of vision.

If you are driving slowly, say five miles an hour, then you need not have intense vigilant focus and you do not need to look five miles ahead as you drive. But as you pick up speed, the faster you drive, the more critical it is to keep your focus. And your focus, along with your depth perception, needs to increase accordingly with velocity as well in driving, as in all of life. Attention to your focus must be maintained at higher speeds if you are to achieve the results you want in life. The faster you are going, the greater and more expanded your depth perception and field of vision need to be, to be optimally effective and most enjoyable.

Fortunately we humans have a guidance device, an inner GPS system, that calls us forward. That small still voice. Listen. You will hear it.

Some call it God, others call it your conscience, some call it your soul. It has been called your life path, your inner knowing, your guidance. Some even call this force science or physics. Whatever you call it, it is our guiding principle. Your gut feeling, the knowing in your heart.

The more sure of yourself you are, the faster you can go, and the more quickly you can achieve desired, joyful results. The less sure or experienced you are, and the faster you go, the scarier it can get, and the results may not be what you want. Let your velocity match your confidence levels. As you gain experience, greater clarity, and see with greater depth and expanded vision, velocity will increase naturally to your new set point. It won't be scary - it will be organic, comfortable and even expected.

You will expect to succeed, you will expect to be at your destination or goal sooner rather than later.

History, Her-Story and Their Story

If you look in the direction of history, then you are bound to repeat it. Because you are focusing on it. It is part of the fabric of energy that you are broadcasting. And what we focus on, we see.

So, before you start walking or driving down any road, make sure it is the road that your soul is calling you toward. Onward…

The Human GPS System (God Positioning System)

GPS - Our Eye in the Sky

"GPS satellites circle the earth twice a day in a very precise orbit and transmit signal information to earth. GPS receivers take this information and use triangulation to calculate the user's exact location. Essentially, the GPS receiver compares the time a signal was transmitted by a satellite with the time it was received. The time difference tells the GPS receiver how far away the satellite is. Now, with distance measurements from a few more satellites, the receiver can determine the user's position and display it on the unit's electronic map."

"A GPS receiver must be locked on to the signal of at least three satellites to calculate a 2D position (latitude and longitude) and track movement. With four or more satellites in view, the receiver can determine the user's 3D position (latitude, longitude and altitude). Once the user's position has been determined, the GPS unit can calculate other information, such as speed, bearing, track, trip distance, distance to destination, sunrise and sunset time and more." [25]

GPS, from my perspective, is a genius creation. Most, if not all, technology is based on a concept that exists organically and GPS is no exception. In my car, I can program in where I want to go, my desired destination, and the marvelous GPS will tell me every step of the way where I am in relation to my destination, the quickest way to get there, points of interest along the way (fun, attractions, eats, fuel), and will guide me to where I want to go.

Linda LaFlamme

3D Vision - *Triangulation provides a perceptual framework and allows a position to be identified.*

The more vantage points from which we look, the clearer the pathway from which we can see. Just as triangulation allows for an assessment of position in relation to destination it works symbolically in the same way with our human technology. With human technological triangulation with your GPS (God Positioning System), the components

138

are our heart, mind and eyes. Our physical eyes are connected with a wider perceptual station of our eyes in the sky, our greater mind. This wider perspective is shone through our minds' eyes and produces the projection that we see and experience here on this earth.

GPS never tells you where your destination *should* be or roguishly programs in a destination. That is up to you and you alone. You must decide where you want to go, your destination. You get to choose from an infinite world of possibilities. All you need to do is head in the direction that it offers you, after you've made your clear choice where you want to go. You keep your eyes on the road in that direction and if you veer away or take a detour, it will recalculate based on where you are at that point in time, your coordinates. There is no wrong place to be. You are always in the right place. You can get to where you want to be from anywhere. There is a Point A, your starting point, and a Point B, destination. There are no wrong turns. If you take a turn that is not on your intended course, just listen to GPS (God Positioning System), it will get you back on course.

This is similar to the function of our minds. Your brilliant, thinking mind - it needs to be programmed by you to where you want to go. It first requires a decision and then requires your vision and focus. Oftentimes our minds have been programmed by something outside of us, our parents, society, others in our lives with their own specific desires for us, such as how we should behave, act and who they think we should be or become. Sometimes our minds can run amok with random programs that we have exposed

ourselves to, a type of mind-software virus, perhaps
negative stories that may not be true or preferred, negative
dramas, fear-based emanations from fearful but perhaps
well-meaning friends or society.

And what is truth anyway?

Truth is your reality, what you make real. This is what is
true for you. Truth is subjective. Someone else's truth is not
your truth necessarily and vice versa. Truth is what you
have made real, projected, to see.

What about what appears fixed? When we springboard and
reach new levels of understanding, new evolutionary
thought levels, then we "see" things in a different way. A
new truth is born. We see and experience different things.
A different world is realized. Made real. Becomes reality.

But, back to our inner GPS...

Regarding GPS, to get to the destination that you want to
go to, you must decide where it is you want to go, and then
program or reprogram your inner computer (mind) to the
destination of your choice. On my vehicle's GPS it is very
easy. I press 'Cancel Current Destination', and then press
'Enter New Destination'. It is really also that simple in our
actual lives. Decision, focus, travel. Start where you are.
Then turn and head in that direction, the direction of your
best life and for those whom you love. Your guidance (God
Positioning System) will tell you the rest.

And it will recalculate along each step of the way, based on your chosen turns.

Decision > Focus > Travel

Journey > Enjoyment > Destiny

What is my Destination or Destiny?

Many people go through life without stopping at intervals to ask themselves this basic question. To stop and look where it is that they are going and to assess the trajectory that they are traveling on, the direction that they are headed in if they stay on the exact same course. Perhaps it is because we have been taught to believe that something else, someone else, the weather, the Point A , our starting point, ...decides our fate, our destination, our destiny.

Point A is only your starting point. It has nothing to do, really, with the direction in which you intend to head in. Point B is there for you, calling you. Move forward... with deliberate focus and love. You don't have to run or drive fast - just turn toward Point B and your inner GPS will take you there. You don't even need to make up for perceived "lost" time. Just enjoy the journey. The journey is the fun of getting there. The joy is in the journey.

JOurneY

Questions to ask yourself along the journey:
-If I stay on this course, where will it lead?

-Is this where I want to be? Is this the trajectory I want to be on?
-Where do I want to go? Where is my heart, mind, body and soul calling me toward?

What happens when the destination you want to head in is not recognized by those that you know? Or it is a path that you have not heard of yet?

Congratulations, you are in visionary territory! You have an uncharted route. A new way. A new path. It is up to you to create it and then leave breadcrumbs for others to tread this new path, this new way.

Much like other visionaries as Sir Richard Branson when he started Virgin Group, or Jeff Bezos conceiving the worlds largest virtual bookstore and more, Mark Zuckerberg, Sergey Brin and Larry Page, Elon Musk, and countless other brilliant visionaries of our modern day.

Different Views for Every Human Being

This world is made up of over seven billion people with seven billion different fields of vision and levels of vision, all seeing things differently, seeing different things.

Through our beliefs, we see in our minds and replay in our thoughts how we think the world is. Then from our beliefs, our thoughts create the world that supports our beliefs. First we believe it, then we see it. We envision our personal worlds into being.

Remember our discussion on Thought-Habit-Belief-Pattern (T-H-B-P). This is how many if not most of your beliefs came into being. Conscious and unconscious habits and patterns. Some were passed along to you through osmosis when you were very young. When we were more recorders than projectors, we had more of a blank canvas. These are only learned ways of being, no right or wrong, no shame or guilt, as these or any negative emotions will not improve your vision. In fact, they, the negative or unpleasant emotions, will do the opposite and keep any unhealthy, non productive, static, undesirable beliefs in your thought-world. *Set them free. Alchemize them. Set yourself free.*

When you expand your vision you rise to a new level of seeing, a new vista. The solution to anything does not exist at the altitude of the problem. You rise above and see it from a different vantage point.

To improve your vision you must improve your internal vision, what you envision. If desired, to change your vision, what you see out there, you need to dream a new dream inside, discover a new vision internally. Dream your better life into being. Think your new story into being, replacing that old outdated worn-out tale. We can choose to be a victim. Or we can choose to create our new, better, revised, expanded world, starting now. All we ever have is now. This is your Point A. Where you were before - yesterday, last week, twenty years ago... matters not.

Rightness and Wrongness

If over seven billion people are experiencing over seven billion different versions of a world, who is right?

As citizens of this planet we argue about who is right and who is wrong. "Right" really means your beliefs. "Wrong" is the other person's beliefs that don't quite match the way you are seeing the world. We are all projecting our own set of beliefs out there, and seeing what we believe to be true. Our projections from our minds (T-H-B-P) keep reinforcing our beliefs.

There is not right or wrong, only evolved ways of seeing. Those evolved ways are more expansive and inclusive and colorful than the previous spectrum of view. We can look at history, or what has been taught to us as history through someone's particular lens of vision, and see that we have evolved as a species, our thinking has evolved over time. In my own personal experience I can look back a couple of decades at pop culture and popular ideas and memes and see that we are indeed on an evolutionary path. The internet makes us a more connected global collective than in generations past. It is almost unfathomable to me to understand how racial and gender issues could have existed as they did in the 60s and prior, coming from my now vantage point. I cannot even think at that level of inequality. ... it is not even remotely near my thoughts or beliefs. And would never be a part of my vision. But it was a part of many's vision as a learned behavior pattern. ...I am thankful to live in the now. We are in a different snapshot of time and vantage point. That's evolution of our species.

But it takes a visionary to stand out and make his or her voice heard. It takes one person, one human being to vision a new way about a topic that is important to them, to hold that vision, to put that beautiful and beneficial vision out into the world. *Is this you?*

In the midst of the tumultuous 60s in the USA, Dr. King's *I Have a Dream* speech. Bill Gates' idea of a computer on every desktop in the 1970s. Al Gore inventing the internet ...wait, scratch that one. But seriously, *one* is all that is takes to change the world.

Which topics are important to you? What do you know as an evolutionary way?

Envision your dream. How can you translate your vision into the physical world? Start with your dream, like Dr. King. Or any of the other visionaries of our present and past. Galileo, Elon Musk, ... you?

You are on this list. You are a visionary of the future. I can't wait to see what your loving, beautiful and important effects on your world will be.

> *There are no small deeds done with open hearts and minds. Start now...*

Linda LaFlamme

Follow Your Heart, It Knows the Way

Just as our vehicle's GPS has several components (receiver, satellites, control segment, etc.), our internal GPS components consists of several parts; These are our minds, our heart, our gut, and our vision.

Our vision tells us where we want to go. This is what we are requesting from our internal GPS.

So, our vision is programmed into the GPS, then our thinking minds do their part to compute logical scenarios and paths. The signal is then connected with the satellites in the sky, our higher selves, source, the help in the ethers. Our consciousness beams back down the signal to our brains telling us to go this way, do that, meet this person, go in that direction.

How do we know that we are going the right way? Our hearts are our compass, our guiding force in concert with our minds. Our hearts along with our gut feelings are our physical sensing instruments. If you feel it in your gut, or feel it in your heart, you will know the answer. Ask any business visionary and they will tell you that they make gut decisions. The more connected you are with your humanity, your gut, your heart - the more potent and more expansive vision you can realize. You are spirit in matter after all, matter in spirit.

Your heart knows the way. It always has. Often, we had this trained or even beaten out of us since we were small

146

children. We were told, "Be a man." or "Boys don't cry.", teaching us to not feel and thus to move away from our own navigation system, just because some external person did not want to deal with us crying. We were also told, "Get over it.", and other harmful projections from well-meaning people who may have been hurt and had their emotions bottled up so they wanted you to not be hurt in life and showed you the only way they knew how to deal with it.

If this is the case, do you think it is maybe time to break this chain of disconnection from yourself. Otherwise you are likely to repeat the mistakes of the past. And wonder why you are not getting different results. And then thinking that the world is this way. ...when it is just your vision that needs adjustment. Adjustment in the direction of what you want, of a better life for you and for those important to you.

Sometimes we have been so beaten down with dogma, circumstance, old ways, that we have lost connection with our hearts. We don't even know how to begin to tune in. But no matter how disconnected we have become, that flicker in our hearts, that flame, is always there. It remains a quiet burning constant while we are alive in this beautiful life that we are given to create the way we want.

It is helpful to remember a time in your life when you felt very connected with your heart, with yourself. Replay that in your mind. What was the circumstance? How old were you? How did that feel? Remember this feeling. This is the feeling of your inner vision. The vision that is unique to you. Your unique brand of magic, that is meant for you to express and live.

When we live our vision, it is joyous. When we can connect with that feeling in our heart, in our gut, that guides us in the right direction, we experience revelations and a-ha's. This is how evolutionary ideas are born or discovered.

Remember that flicker in your heart. Your dreams, your visionary path. When you can feel it and see it, then put your focus on it. This flicker will expand into a flame. The flame in your heart is what keeps you alive and engaged in life. This sacred connection within you is with you always. It is your connection to yourself, your higher self, source, god, however you want to view it in the larger sense.

When we are divorced from our hearts, all measures of calamity can exist in our world. We are missing an entire component of our GPS, the one that tells us if we are going in the best direction for us. How do you know that you are on the right track? Because it feels good to you. It brings relief. It makes you smile. You feel it in your gut that you are now pointing in the right direction. Degrees of evolution are based on your field of vision (short or expansive), your clarity, and your focus.

If you follow your heart, and have a clear connection to your personal meaning and vision, you would never create ill will against anyone. Because your thinking is visionary, expansive, and evolutionary, you recognize "them" as part of you.

When someone is said to be brilliant, it is the result of their heart and mind, working in concert, in symphony with their own personal greater vision so that they can express themselves in high-impact ways, miraculous to many (those who have not yet learned how vision truly works). One's brilliance in this world can outshine exponentially any mediocrity that is dimly projecting. How many lives have our visionary leaders touched - millions... billions? How many lives will you affect in a positive manner? Day by day. One by one.

Be brilliant. Shine your brilliant self.

But, even if you touch only one life with your brilliance you can feel reward. For it is your expression itself that is the gift.

The more clarity we see with, and the more expansive our field of vision and depth perception, the more inclusive we understand the world to be.

Evolution or Creation?

Our Eyes of God provide creation. And then evolution.

First we are born as Recorders. And then we become Projectors.

> *...creation...evolution...creation...evolution...creation... evolution...creation...evolution...>*

Our Eyes of God provide creation. And then evolution.

Linda LaFlamme

Who is the Dreamer? What is the Dream?

Who is the dreamer? Is it you, the human being, who is dreaming your world into being? The you who is envisioning a better future?

You, through all of your unique experiences, journeys, interactions and in your lifetime thus far, have envisioned a new way, the highest and best path and future that you would like to see for yourself, for your life. And this may include the highest and best that you would wish for your family, children, community, and your greater world.

Our desires encompass our immediate range of vision and our vision for a better world.

So, who is the dreamer…

Is it you envisioning? Or is it a higher being, higher power, God, source, physics, something larger than the sum of its parts, envisioning a more evolved world?

I would theorize that the answer is *Yes*. To both questions.

Thoughts… we catch them, we tune into the frequency of them, and then can comprehend them, see new ways. We then give them life, make them real, make them manifest.

They arise from our perspective, our unique angle, our view of the world. And the way that what we see would be improved if we brought this vision into being.

But I think there is another part to this formula.

150

Often the endpoints will call us in a particular way if we listen to our inner guidance. I have long pondered the question: Am I creating the journey? Or am I being pulled into the journey by the destination, the surprise ending? I think the answer is both. I feel that we set our coordinates and then off we go in the direction of our chosen journey. The journey is a delight and we get to create each step. We are heading in a specific direction as that is where we are looking, where our focus is. Our destination is the endpoint, the Point B that we are heading toward. Although in actuality all endpoints are really resting points to savor because the delicious journey never truly ends there. It continues forward with refined visions and new, expanded horizons.

If you are a visionary with evolutionary thoughts, ways, ideas that would benefit you, your family, your company, your industry, or even humanity…*and you are*… then there is something greater calling you forward. The greatest visionaries of our world produce benefit for all who realize the fruits of their vision.

We dream the dream. And we dream the dreamer.

Our desires, that small still voice inside, our dreams, our visions of a better life, situation or world, our souls, call us in a direction that is unique, special to us and to the extent that we allow ourselves to hear it, our ride can be slow or fast, bumpy or delicious. It's a matter of hearing or seeing and focus.

We embark on new journeys and we never quite know what will happen. This is the fun of it all. We get to delight in the discovery of our own journey, our own path. Who we are.

We get to decide our fate. How much happiness we allow in is entirely up to us on an individual level.

All we need to do is tune in to what we really want inside and head toward that direction. Our inner GPS (God Positioning System) will guide us there. The rest we can create along the way.

And this is the best and most juicy, delectable part... I feel that it is not even about the endpoints. These points on a line summon us, beckon to us. And we choose the route that we will take. It is really about the journey itself. This is the delicious part, the best part.

Make it the most enjoyable journey possible for yourself. Because it is not about the destination. It is about the fun along the way.

We dream the dream. And we dream the dreamer.

What is the Dream?

The more you connect with yourself, tune into yourself, discover who you *really* are, your unique being, the more you can express yourself fully. And then you oftentimes become the influencer in your sphere or specialty.

The greatest of leaders will point the way - the way for those traveling the same road - to look inward, to find themselves, thus the way for all to achieve their own dreams.

The greatest of leaders don't create followers. The greatest of leaders create leaders.

This is true in business, this is true in personal circles and families, and this is true in nations.

Be the leader in your own life. Be the captain of your ship, the creator of your destiny.

It is all up to you. *Where would you like to go?*

Chapter Four: Seeing Through your Eyes of God:
Questions and Exercises

- Who are you? What is your character? Describe in detail who your character is. It may be useful to think back to and through different stages of your life and describe each.

- What are you about? What is important to you?

- Why is your character here? *...Do that. Be you. Fully.*

- What is your future story? *Write it now.*

- What is the setting? Who is the supporting cast? What adventures are included in your story? What goals do you have? What would be the happiest ending to your story (at least for Book One)? You can write Book Two or beyond later after you reach this particular happy ending.

CHAPTER 5
The God Within

A Full Chalice

Are you full of yourself? You certainly should strive to be.

When a person has strayed so far from their course of a happy life, we sometimes say, a popular saying, that they are a mere shell of themselves. They are a body but their soul is not readily apparent. Their experience of joy or love has dimmed. They cannot distinguish or have lost their desires for this life. Well, actually, nothing is ever lost, they just can't see them ("see" them) at the moment, or the month, or year, or decade.

I know as I have been there in my dark years in my teens after my parents had died and again when I was very ill after grad school and this is not a pleasant place to be. Maybe this has happened to you at one point or another in your life. I had lost myself because…. I was taught to look outside of myself for me, who I was, my definition of myself, and my worth in the world.

We can never find the correct answer to the question "Who am I?" out there. You may seek all you want. Your external environment may provide clues. But your path can only be found within. There are markers on your way, but even these are put out there on your path by you, your higher knowing, your soul.

When we describe someone as being "full of themselves" we often compute that to be negative because of learned responses.

When in actuality, being full of yourself is a very good thing! It means that you are more of who you are. And you are here to unabashedly and joyfully express that glorious *you* in this lifetime. The spirit that animates your body.

Shine Your Brilliance

Vision with our eyes and minds determines what we can see in the physical world. It is our dreams and our thought-world, conscious or subconscious, made manifest, as adults.

Vision from within our soul is what we, in our deepest desires and in our hearts, really want to see manifest in this world, in our worlds.

Visionary leaders and creators connect deeply with their soul vision and feel it into being. They make manifest what they can imagine. They create serendipitous situations in their thoughts and minds and thus see them materialize in the physical world. They hold that vision, their inner vision, until it is an outer vision. Made manifest through their Eyes.

Light and Darkness

As you recall from our blind spot discussion... lack of light-receptor cells in a specific area produces a blind spot in our vision. And likewise, when we do not see with enough light in a particular area, then the world appears as dark in that area, metaphorically speaking.

It's not that it *is* dark. It is that it appears dark. To us. That is, we cannot see it in all of its lighted glory.

We see best with our physical eyes when there is more light available. Our human nighttime vision is not quite as keen as our daytime vision. Quite simply, when there is more light shone upon a subject, the more you can see of it, the better it is understood, the more it is illuminated, and the more it stands out for the world. And this applies to people also.

When an object or subject is hidden in the shadows, when it is not illuminated, you cannot see it very well. It does not stand out in the sun. There may be a reason, according to the person, I mean *object*, why it is hidden in the shadows. If there was never an abundance of light shone upon an object, I mean *person*, how would it know its brilliance? If it was in an area, or family, that was only dimly lit with hope, desire, joy and freedom, then it sees itself as dim, not as bright as other objects or subjects that are out in the sun. Shining away.

But how to change this to illuminate your world and your self?

Shining Light in Your Life

When the light is shone upon you, not only do people see you more clearly for who you really are, but also you feel as though you are basking in the sun.

157

Part of my greatest joy is to shine the light in my own individual way, shine a loving gaze, a smile, to those whom I interact with on a daily basis in my travels, so that people in my world see themselves for all of the brilliance that they truly are reflected to them, even if just for a moment or a passing glance. My deep desire is for you to realize your true brilliance. Standing out, shining, leading by example, being a visionary, living your dreams. This is not meant for just a handful of those in the world, but for you. This is why you are reading this book, because you are able to see, you do not have a blind spot to your greatest life, and you have that vision inside of you.

How do we heal the world? Shine the light in the dark corners. Now that you realize how brilliant you really are, despite what you may have been told, heard, or experienced, if you experienced negative, dark, dimly lit projections of others on your journey. Shine the light so that whatever was hidden is illuminated, thus accepted, integrated and whole. To make your world the best that it can be, this is your task. For no one can do it for you. And by light I mean the gaze of your expanded vision. Your Eyes of God.

Where, in your life, can you shine some light? Are there situations that you don't want to see, have not integrated, have not accepted? Which direction do you want to look in? See *yourself* with your Eyes of God. Expand yourself through your Eyes of God.

Shine the light onto *them* and see them, even if they have been "an elephant in the room", for what they are - unique gifts to you to make you smarter, better, and stronger.

Everything in life can be seen as a gift. If you realize the gift within the circumstance, situation or person. For example, in my life, I began working summer and school vacations at age twelve to pay for my school clothes and other expenses. At the time I could not see the gift in it. But, I learned that it had great value in teaching me of the importance of work, the value of my time, working in the smartest way possible, the value of balance and fun, and it prepared me for success. I feel that Larry Ellison would agree. And I feel that Oprah would smile with knowing. As Steve Jobs would have. Even though Point A seemed difficult, it provided internal strength and fortitude.

If it doesn't kill you, it makes you stronger.

The Light Source - Where Does it Originate From?

Technology, Art, and Making Movies

Genius exists in the creative world of filmmaking, creative storytelling brought to life on screens large and small. From the screenwriters, artists, actors, directors, designers, producers, creatives, and all involved in every aspect of this craft, vision is demonstrated and illustrated, as this is the art of creating a world and making it manifest. And then sharing it with others.

Within this field, a story with characters, a focus and locus, a world unto itself, has been envisioned, created, translated and brought to life through the magic of a medium with synergistic co-creation. The finished world is then projected in a technological way, much like our biological computers, our own vision, as a reality that we see out there - on a screen of our choosing.

And as human Projectors, we do the same. Only our screen is our world that we see and experience.

The Movie Projector

Before digital, the first movie projectors relied on shining a light on static images that were moved along in front of the light at a certain base speed to produce the illusion of a movement of story.

A movie projector is a device that continuously moves film along a path so that each frame of the film is stopped for a fraction of a second in front of a light source. The light source provides extremely bright illumination that casts the image on the film through a lens onto a screen.

This is how our lives work as well. The light source is what is behind our eyes. Our Eyes. The greater light source. This greater source is us in our totality.

The story of our lives appears on the screen in front of us, the screen that we call our world.

The frames of film are the moments of our lives. Time provides the container for our moments and the rhythm to become a cohesive story, narrative, drama, fairy tale or legend. Single moments weave the fabric of our tale.

When we switch off the light, the movie or story has ended. While the light source is on, we experience our story based on the technology and the input. The technology is our Eyes of God, our Projector system that includes our brain and eye systems, our hearts, and our minds. This works in direct connection with our GPS and the quality of the lens of our perception and how well we continuously write and rewrite our script of the screenplay tale.

Persistence of Vision

Reality is merely an illusion, albeit a very persistent one.
   Albert Einstein

The Big Movie Screen

Our lives and reality "out there" are similar to a large movie screen projection from our minds, our thoughts, our likes, our dislikes, our hopes, our fears. And everyone is watching a different movie. Some slightly different and some vastly different. Some, most, are dramas, some are tragedies and some are comedies. It is all a matter of which movie is being played, or what story is loaded in the projector (of your mind, your eye/brain system), your thoughtworld, or said in another way, what you are inside that is projected onto the outside. Your beliefs, your wishes, your triumphs, your habits, and your patterns.

The light is within us, the light behind our eyes, the light that we project out onto the world and see as "out there".

The more dim or obscured our visions, our light, the more dim our world will be. Appearing darker, less light. When we don't let our full light shine through, we see the world as shadows, fears, shapes rather than clearly delineated thoughts or joyful, potent manifestations. We see merely a small percentage of the power and glory that we really are.

We do not see people or situations as they are, we see them as we are.

So what we are seeing out there, we are actually projecting out there. Because we see people as we are, not as they are. In fact, we see everything as we are, not as it is. And we all have our own angles and points of view from which to see. This is the beauty of life on this earth - we have over seven billion points of view. And all of them are valid, all of them are right, in an individual sense.

The Characters in our Movie (Our World)

Character

What is "character"? It is the unique expression of us that our storyline builds in our worldly experience. We can say that, "He has good character" or exclaim, "What a character!". The latter meaning, he is probably full of himself - which is actually a great thing. But what does this mean? The closer we are to our individual true nature and expressing our unique essence, the deeper our character is developed and expressed.

We "build character" through our experiences, particularly the challenging ones.

But just who is this "character"? It is our unique expression. We are playing our part on this world stage. We are all characters in a drama, interweaving stories and experiences. Co-creating and participating in a journey that is evolving to an ever finer degree. Are there any bad characters? Well, we have characters that we prefer to meet or interact with and characters that we don't. And these are subjective. The billionaire businessman and the Himalayan monk's paths may never cross, and this may be fine for both of them - it is a matter of frequency and desires. Who is right and who is wrong... Is the monk? Is the businessman? They are only "in character" playing their parts. Being who they are.

Who has an easier time in this earthly experience here - the businessman or the monk? It depends on how you view the situation and from which angle you are looking from and relating to. Praying and meditation for ten hours a day might be pain for the billionaire. And the trappings of wealth, excitement and stimulation of global success may represent pain to the monk. Who is right?

We can't change who we are at our essence. We can't change to please anyone. And why would we want to? Your personality is unique to you. You have God given talents. Your point of view is needed here, this is why you were born. Embrace it. Love it. Express it.

Your point of view is needed here, this is why you were born.

Interaction builds our character.

We are inspired to want what we want. We cannot change what we want or what we desire. It simply is. It is a by-product of our experiences to date and our thought mind data-crunching in concert with our heart wisdom.

We get to prove to ourselves who we are, what we are made of, and then make further refining choices, based on our preferences.

Character Arc

Characters grow and evolve as the story unfolds. Your character builds as you continue on the path of life. Your character, that is, *you*, become more specific about your desires, your needs, your path in life. It becomes clear to you at some point, the path that you need to take. Oh, you can ignore it for a year or decades or longer, but it is there tapping you on the shoulder. Until you can't ignore it, your path, any longer.

All good stories need a path to carry you along, a drama, a goal to head toward, a protagonist, a hero, and an antagonist, a seeming impediment to the hero's journey to help you grow and expand your vision, build your strengths.

The farther in depth you go, inner exploring outer, as your visionary self, the finer the levels you can discern. So instead of having a dramatic unpleasant event happen to point us in our desired direction, we see finer levels to make course corrections. We follow our gut more. We have a greater field of vision. We understand more. So instead of tragedies we experience more refinement.

These turning points appear, instead of crises, as choices or variety. As different paths or options. This door or that door. We can see and sense them sooner on the trajectory and modify choices and make course corrections as we go. Rather than being "blindsided" by an event. As you increase and expand your vision, you decrease your chances of "blind spots" or of being "blindsided".

> If you're not the hero in your story, rewrite your story!

> *You are the author of your life's narrative. What story do you want to tell?*

- Are you the hero in your story?

- Or do you look to another character to be the hero?

- Is there an antagonist in your story? Or many? Or multiple antagonists antagonizing you about the same issue?

- How will you grow from this to arrive at the happy ending?

> *The eyes are the windows to the soul. Really.*

Visionaries Change the World

Visionaries, those who can see with expanded vision, have led the way for change and have inspired countless others as a beacon of light.

Throughout history and in our modern day, global visionaries and luminaries have lit the way for advancement and evolution. At just the right times, they have stepped into their rightful place of leadership in a world yearning for revolutionary ideas and practice. When our world needed them most, they appeared with a new idea, a new way, a new vision. It has been said that when the student is ready the teacher appears, this is true on the global scale as well as in individuals' lives.

These visionaries may have not realized their destiny as teachers when they started their path. They just had an idea, a vision, that needed to be borne unto this world. Something was calling them toward a path, tapping them on the shoulder, whispering in their ear.

Is this you?

How Visionaries See and Create the World

There are eight steps to realizing your vision or to creating heaven on earth.

**8 Steps to Realizing Your Vision
and Seeing Your Creation**
or, said in another way,
8 Steps to Heaven on Earth

1. *Desire* - It all begins with desire. Everything begins with desire.
2. *Imagine* - From desire, you discern and become inspired.
3. *Envision* - Seed of an idea in your mind's eye.
4. *Translate*- Feel the emotion and texture of the essence of that seed idea.
5. *Create* - Birth of the idea.
6. *Shine* - Emanate, "see it" in your world.
7. *Receive* - Bask in the reflection of your beautifully emanated creation.
8. *Enjoy* - Experience in your heart what you knew could be all along. Savor your role as creator.

You now have the tools. Go forth, you visionary creator. Looking through the Eyes of God.

Go and create your best life. Change *your* world. Change *the* world.

~

I have so enjoyed our journey together and I look forward to more. Thank you for reading as this book was written for you. You now know all of the mechanics of envisioning what you would like to see... and you have yourself uncovered the tools necessary to create the best life possible and radiate the visionary creations within you. Envision your better world into being. Whether you apply this with yourself, as an example with your family, your children, friends, wider circle, or the world. We will all benefit by what you have to offer, that unique blend of qualities and talents and beauty that *you* are inside. I am very grateful for you.

Go forth, you visionary creator, and create your best life.

You are seeing and creating through the Eyes of God.

It is God who is looking through your eyes. Go forth and create a beautiful new world.

> *See what you love, Love what you see.*
> *.... for it is you. Seeing and being seen through the Eyes of God.*

Chapter Five: Knowing Who You Are.
Homework

- Go forth and create your best life.

- Enjoy and savor. Don't forget to play more than work.

- Be Love.

Eyes of God Bibliography and Resources

Chapter One:

1 Observer Effect,
http://en.wikipedia.org/wiki/Observer_effect_(physics)

2 The Pygmalion Effect and the Rosenthal Effect
http://en.wikipedia.org/wiki/Pygmalion_effect

3 The Pygmalion Effect Relative to Schools The Rosenthal
- Jacobson study,
http://en.wikipedia.org/wiki/Pygmalion_effect

Chapter Two:

4 p. Definition of Vision, http://www.merriam-
webster.com/dictionary/vision

Chapter Three:

5 Vision with Our Eyes, Our Eyesight, livescience.com

6 Vision with Our Eyes, Our Eyesight,
http://www.aces.edu/pubs/docs/U/UNP-0066/UNP-
0066.pdf

7 Vision with Our Eyes, Our Eyesight, (https://answers.yahoo.com/question/index?qid=200903071 60837AArGOqJ)

8 Vision with Our Eyes, Our Eyesight, http://en.wikipedia.org/wiki/Hearing_range

9 "How Your Eyes Work" http://www.aoa.org/patients-and-public/resources-for-teachers/how-your-eyes-work

10 "How Your Eyes Work" http://www.aoa.org/patients-and-public/good-vision-throughout-life/childrens-vision/infant-vision-birth-to-24-months-of-age?sso=y

11 Vision Issues and Distortions, Nearsightedness. Source: http://www.aoa.org/patients-and-public/eye-and-vision-problems/glossary-of-eye-and-vision-conditions/myopia

12 Vision Exercises. Visit http://www.LindaLaFlamme.com or http://www.EyesofGodbook.com for information on clarity and vision exercises to help expand your vision.

13 - Farsightedness, Source: http://www.aoa.org/patients-and-public/eye-and-vision-problems/glossary-of-eye-and-vision-conditions/hyperopia

14 - Blurred Vision, http://www.aoa.org/patients-and-public/eye-and-vision-problems/glossary-of-eye-and-vision-conditions/astigmatism

15 - Vision and Age, http://www.webmd.com/eye-health/tc/farsightedness-hyperopia-topic-overview

16 - The Different Way of Interpreting that we Call Spectrum Disorder
http://en.wikipedia.org/wiki/Stephen_Wiltshire
http://www.youtube.com/watch?v=95L-zmIBGd4

17 - Daniel Tammet,
http://en.wikipedia.org/wiki/Daniel_Tammet

18 Synesthesia, http://www.bu.edu/synesthesia/faq/

19 - Synesthesia, http://en.wikipedia.org/wiki/Synesthesia

Chapter Four:

20 - Creator Attributes,
http://www.forbes.com/sites/kathryndill/2013/09/18/by-their-bootstraps-billionaires-who-started-from-scratch/

21 -Visibility and Invisibility,
http://en.wikipedia.org/wiki/Blind_spot_%28vision%29

22 Blind Spots, Translating Light and Seeing Shadows,
http://en.wikipedia.org/wiki/Photoreceptor_cell

23 Near Death Visions and Experiences,
http://www.near-death.com/muslim.html

24 Near Death Visions and Experiences,
http://www.thedailybeast.com/articles/2013/02/08/is-hell-real-people-who-went-there-say-yes.html

25 GPS - Our Eye in the Sky,
http://www8.garmin.com/aboutGPS/

Chapter Five:

The Movie Projector,
http://entertainment.howstuffworks.com/movie-projector1.htm

About the Author

Linda LaFlamme is an entrepreneur, author and inspirational thought leader. Her interests are focused in leading edge fields and in helping dynamic visionaries and luminaries, innovative businesses and pioneering entrepreneurs utilize all of their unexplored skills and innate resources to tap their creativity and develop new thought platforms and patterns. Linda invites you take a leap of faith to revolutionize your world and live your best life.

Highlights of Linda's career have included founding an automotive consulting company that delivered revolutionary changes in the industry, a wellness and fitness consulting company, and a travel company to sacred sites and adventure destinations. She is also founder of a global wellness association, establishing professional industry standards, a

community learning atmosphere, and progressive objectives for wellness professionals in over 50 countries.

Linda, whose last name does mean "the fire" or "the flame", brings an energy and passion to her inspired work. A common theme in all of her seemingly diverse work is concretizing a vision and creating a platform to make the world a better place, to offer new solutions, and to empower those involved to create their best life. Linda achieves her mission through loving stewardship of her expressions be they businesses or other creative work such as books, music, or film.

Visit www.LindaLaFlamme.com for additional information, articles or to sign up for her newsletter and advanced notices of upcoming books, tour dates, personal messages, and news.

Visit www.LindaLaFlamme.com
Connect facebook.com/LindaLaFlamme.LL
Follow twitter.com/LindaMLaFlamme